Garlic
Nature's Super Healer

❖ JOAN WILEN & LYDIA WILEN ❖

PRENTICE HALL
Paramus, New Jersey 07652

Library of Congress Cataloging-in-Publication Data

Wilen, Joan.
    Garlic : nature's super healer / by Joan Wilen & Lydia Wilen.
      p. cm.
    Includes index.
    ISBN 0-13-522871-9 (case)—ISBN 0-13-522897-2 (pbk.)
    1. Garlic—Therapeutic use. I. Wilen, Lydia. II. Title.
    RM666.G15W55   1997   96-43518
    615′.324324—dc20   CIP

Printed in the United States of America

10 9 8 7 6 5 4 3 2 1   10 9 8 7 6 5 4 3 2 (pbk)

The information presented in this book is designed to help you make informed decisions about your health. It is not intended as a substitute for medical care nor a manual for self-treatment. If you feel that you have a medical problem, seek professional medical advice promptly.

ISBN 0-13-522871-9 (case)

ISBN 0-13-522897-2 (pbk)

PRENTICE HALL
Career & Personal Development
Paramus, NJ 07652
A Simon & Schuster Company

On the World Wide Web at http://www.phdirect.com

Prentice-Hall International (UK) Limited, *London*
Prentice-Hall of Australia Pty. Limited, *Sydney*
Prentice-Hall Canada Inc., *Toronto*
Prentice-Hall Hispanoamericana, S.A., *Mexico*
Prentice-Hall of India Private Limited, *New Delhi*
Prentice-Hall of Japan, Inc., *Tokyo*
Simon & Schuster Asia Pte. Ltd., *Singapore*
Editora Prentice-Hall do Brasil, Ltda., *Rio de Janeiro*

What This Book Can Do For You

By the time you finish reading this book, you will be able to answer the question, "If you could take only one herb with you to that proverbial desert island, which would it be?" (Not that anyone is going to ask you that question or that you need to plan for the trip to that desert island.) But without even reading this book, you know, of course, that garlic should be the answer.

Forget the desert island! Deal with your life as it is wherever it is and let this book teach you how garlic can improve specific health challenges, your sense of well-being, your home-cooked meals, your pet's health, and even your living conditions (especially if you have an ant problem).

Garlic can make a real difference in the way you feel, your energy level, your memory. It can help strengthen your immune system, prevent serious heart problems by lowering cholesterol and blood pressure, and can help prevent blood clots and strokes. Using the expertise of doctors, herbalists, alternative and complementary health professionals, scientific researchers, and folk medicine handed down from generation to generation, we've gathered this collection of simple, effective, and inexpensive garlic remedies.

There are ways to reap the rewards of eating raw garlic without any of the harsh side effects—no burning pain, no garlic breath. And we happily share it all with you in this book. We also tell you how to buy garlic supplements and the important words to look for on a label.

Do you have a dog, a bird, a horse, or are you a cat person? We have remedies for keeping your pet from needing a vet.

Got a green thumb? Well, whatever color it is, it's easy to grow garlic, and this book tells you how. You can also grow garlic greens in a week or two that you can toss into a salad for some extra oomph. Incidentally, you don't need a farm or a big garden. Apartment dwellers can get in on the action, too.

For your amusement, there are fun and fascinating facts, folk legends, quotes, and a few dozen ways to say garlic in other languages. For your ordering pleasure, you'll want to check out the Resources section and call for some free catalogs.

Once you really get into garlic—if you haven't already—you'll want to know about the Garlic Festivals. We've gathered the most comprehensive list around.

Getting hungry? Our selection of recipes is very special, each containing garlic, of course. And the variety of dishes is extraordinary, as are the chefs who shared their recipes with us.

Meanwhile, back to that proverbial desert island—is there any question that garlic is the answer? Garlic—a natural antibiotic with antiviral, antifungal, anticoagulant, and antiseptic properties—can act as an expectorant and decongestant, antioxidant, germicide, anti-inflammatory agent, diuretic, sedative, and it is believed to contain cancer-preventive chemicals. Besides all that, it's also said to be an aphrodisiac. To replenish your supply, you simply plant some of its own cloves, and this beautiful bulb clones itself!

So, what this book can do for you is to let you know what *garlic* can do for you. And that can be a whole lot!

Table of Contents

What This Book Can Do For You   /   iii

Acknowledgments   /   xii

Introduction   1

No Matter How You Say It . . . Garlic in 45 Languages   /   4

Garlic's "Believe It or Not"   7

Garlic As Medicine   19

General Dosage: Internal Use   22

General Dosage: External Use   22

What to Take, How, and Why   23

The Secret of Selecting the Best Supplements   24

General Tips   24

Seven Easy Ways to Eat Raw Garlic   25

Remedies   29

AIDS . . . Strengthening the Immune System   31

Allergies . . . Garlic to the Rescue!   31

Anemia . . . Nature's Blood Builder   32

Animal Bites . . . First-Aid Kit in a Bulb   33

Arteriosclerosis and Atherosclerosis . . . Nature's Own Blood Thinner   34

Arthritis . . . Soothing Relief With Garlic   34

Asthma . . . Breathe Freer and Easier   35

Blisters . . . Rub Away Discomfort   36

Blood . . . and the Blood-Building Power of Garlic   37

*Blood Clots . . . For Prevention: Move Over Aspirin—Here's
    Garlic!   37*

Blood pressure . . . The Great Equalizer   38

Body Odor (from garlic) . . . Soak Away the Smell   41

Breast-Feeding (Nursing) . . . Whet Baby's Appetite   41

Bronchitis . . . Calm the Cough; Clear Up the Condition   41

Burns (minor ones only)   41

*Cancer . . . Prevention and Treatment: New Hope With
    Garlic   42*

*Cholesterol . . . Raise the Good (HDL);
    Lower the Bad (LDL)   43*

Colds/Flu . . . Making Them Yesterday's News   44

Cold Sores . . . Rapid Relief   47

Colitis . . . Remarkable Regularity Restorer   47

Congestion . . . Nature's Roto Rooter   47

Constipation . . . The Stimulating Power of Allicin   48

*Coughs . . . Healing Homemade Soup, Syrup, Tea,
    and Lozenges   48*

Cystitis . . . The Magic of Nature's Own Infection Fighter   49

Depression . . . Garlic for a Natural High   49

Diabetes . . . Blood-Sugar Level Reducer   50

*Diarrhea and Dysentery . . . Fast-Acting Stopper
    and Preventative   50*

*Digestion and Indigestion . . . Digestive-Enzyme
    Stimulator   52*

Dysbiosis (Leaky Gut Syndrome) . . . Heartburn Helper   52

Ears . . . Garlic: In One Ear and Out the Other   53

*Eye Spots . . . Helpful Vitamin-Absorbing
    Power of Garlic   55*

Fatigue . . . A Wake-up Sniff and Drink   55

Feet . . . Heal Heels, Toes, and a Corn That Grows   56

Fever . . . Bringing It Down With Sole Food   57

*Fingernails . . . Put an End to Thin, Breaking,
    and Splitting Nails   58*

*Gangrene . . . Emergency Measures to Save Life
and/or Limb* 58

Garlic Breath . . . Fifteen Ways to De-Garlic Breath 59

*Gout . . . Out! Out! Damned Gout With an Eating
Regimen* 60

*Gum Problems (Gingivitis) . . . A Remedy to Sink Your
Teeth Into* 61

Hair . . . Garlic for Your Crowning Glory 61

Hangover . . . Symptom-Easing Gazpacho 62

Hay Fever . . . Do-the-Trick Nosedrops 64

Headache . . . Using Nature's Aspirin 64

Heart . . . Garlic: The Smart-Heart Herb 65

*Hemorrhoids . . . A Clove a Day Where the Sun
Don't Shine* 66

*Hepatitis . . . Prevention and Treatment Until
You Get Help* 66

Herpes . . . Nature's Preventative 67

Immune System . . . A Three-Ingredient Power Potion 67

Impetigo . . . Fast Healing Relief 68

*Impotence . . . A Simple Test and a Stimulating
Treatment* 68

Infections . . . Garlic, the Supreme Combatant 70

Insect Bites . . . Stop the Itching; Start the Healing 71

Insect Repellent . . . The Great Shoo-er 71

*Insomnia . . . A Relaxing Lead-In to a Good
Night's Z-Z-Z-Z* 72

Jock Itch . . . Destroying the Fungus Among Us 73

*Lead Poisoning and Other Heavy Metals . . . Important
Detox Program for the Entire Family* 73

*Liver Disease Prevention . . . Drinking a Daily Liver
Flush* 74

*Lyme Disease . . . Possible Prevention That's Worth
a Try* 74

Mastitis . . . Enhanced Garlic Formula 75

Melanoma . . . Can't Argue With Success 75

Memory . . . A First Lady's Extraordinary-Memory Secret 77

Menopause . . . Symptom-Easing Relief 77

Menstruation . . . Monthly Management 77

Muscle Soreness and Stiffness (Charley Horse) . . . Wash Away Pain 78

Muscle Spasms . . . Easing the Tension 78

Nasal Congestion . . . Clearing the Passages With Fumes 78

Neck . . . Getting Rid of the Pain in the Neck 79

Nervous Tension/Stress . . . Chill Out, Naturally 79

Nightmares (children's) . . . An Intriguing Remedy That Works Like a Dream 80

Nosebleed . . . Garlic—And Step on It! 80

Pneumonia . . . What to Do Until the Doctor Comes 80

Poison Ivy . . . Stop the Itching; Start the Healing 81

Pollution . . . What You Should Know If You Breathe Outdoors 82

Pregnancy . . . More Stamina, Easier Delivery— And a Second Opinion 82

Prostate . . . Infection Protection 83

Psoriasis . . . Juice Your Way to Relief 84

Ringworm . . . A Potent Cleanser 84

Sciatica . . . Five Ways to Be Pain-Free 84

Sinus . . . Nosedrops to Shock Your System 85

Sneezing . . . Keeping You Out of the Record Books 86

Sore Throat . . . The Cause and the Cure 86

Stroke Prevention . . . An Excellent Daily Elixir 88

Sunburn/Windburn . . . Take Tea and See 88

Thrush . . . Thrash Thrush in a Rush 88

Toenail Fungus . . . Nail the Problem With an Anti-Fungal Drink 89

Toothache . . . Ease the Pain; Fight the Infection 89

Vaginal Itching . . . Douche Away Discomfort 90

Warts . . . A Twilight Zone *Treatment That Works* 90

Weight Control . . . A Stop-the-Craving Cocktail 91

Worms . . . Test, Treatment, Prevention 91

Wounds . . . The Fastest and Finest First Aid 92

Yeast Infection (Candida albicans) . . . Symptoms and Suggestions for Men As Well As Women 94

Garlic Remedies for Your Pet / 96

Dosage   96

Appetite Restorer (Horses)   96

Arthritis   96

Bird Mites   97

Cancer   97

Constipation (Horses)   97

Coughs (Dogs)   98

Coughs (Horses)   98

Diet (Cats and Dogs)   98

Ear Mites (Cats and Dogs)   100

Eczema (Cats and Dogs)   100

Fleas, Lice, and Ticks (Cats and Dogs)   100

Infections (Cats and Dogs)   101

Insect Bites (Cats and Dogs)   101

Jaundice (Cats and Dogs)   101

Mange (Cats and Dogs)   102

Tonic (Cats and Dogs)   102

Worms (Cats and Dogs)   102

Health-Giving Garlic Preparations   103

Nature's Amazing Antibiotic   105

Garlic Baths for Restoring Health   106

Enema . . . Nature's Special Cleanser   107

Footbath . . . For a Treatment and a Treat   107

*Garlic Water . . . Combining Nature's Two Miraculous
    Healers   108*

Juice . . . A Potent Potable   108

Oil . . . A Versatile Internal/External Healing Blend   110

Poultice . . . A Remedy for Remarkable Results   111

Soothing Garlic Syrups   112

Tea . . . Decoction and Infusion   114

Tonic . . . To Wake Up "Tired Blood"   116

Vinegar and Garlic . . . Skin Saver   117
Wash and Liniment . . . Internal/External Healer   117

Growing Garlic   119

When to Plant   121
Growing Conditions   122
Garlic As a Companion Plant   122
What to Plant   123
How Much to Plant   124
Planting Nature's Gift   124
Mulching . . . Mother Earth's Blanket   125
Four Important Growing Tips   125
Harvesting . . . Reaping the Rewards   125
Curing . . . Garlic's Coming of Age   126
Garlic Greens . . . Vitality Sprouts   126
Garlic Pesticide   127

Garlic As Food   129

Preparation Tips   131
Nutritional Values   138

Recipes   139

Appetizers   141
Beans and Grains   147
Beef, Pork, and Lamb   152
Breads, Muffins, Clouds, and Croutons   158
Chicken   165
Fish and Seafood   173
Pasta   178
Soups   183
Spreads, Sauces, Dips, Dressings, and a Rub   188

Sweet Treats and Snacks   200
Tofu   206
Vegetables   209

Appendices   225

Garlic Festivals   /   227
Resources   /   230
*Garlic Seed Foundation: Garlic Products . . . Mail Order
    Companies and Stores   232*
Garlic Lovers Association 233

Bibliography   /   234

Index   237

Acknowledgments

BIG THANKS to—

- Douglas Corcoran, our editor, who planted the idea of a garlic book, helped us cultivate it, and patiently awaited the harvest.
- Zsuzsa Neff, Elizabeth Torjussen, Audrey Kopciak, and all other helping hands at Prentice Hall
- Garlic Festival people for their cookbooks, contacts, and friendship: Catherine Veneiro, Father Bill Sangiovanni, Scott Osborn, Richard J. Nicholls, Margaret Leitch, Phyllis Knight, Richard Kappler, D.C., Richard Hanson, Val Filice, Mara Farrell
- Health professionals, research scientists, educators, herbalists, and garlic growers and sellers for sharing their precious time and valuable information: Irwin Ziment, M.D., Ray C. Wunderlich, Jr., M.D., Andrew Weil, M.D., Michael J. Wargovich, Ph.D., Professor Ron Voss, Professor Varro E. Tyler, Master Herbalist Lalitha Thomas, David Stern of the Garlic Seed Foundation, Master Herbalist Debra St. Claire, Botanical Researcher-Herbalist Paul Schulick, Tom Reed of Garlic Festival Foods, Fred Pescatore, M.D., Barbara Levine, M.D., Larry D. Lawson, Ph.D., Ronald Hoffman, M.D., Alan Hirsch, M.D., Chrisy Gustafson of Progressive International Corp., Ann Louise Gittleman, M.S., C.N.S., Ron Engeland of Filaree Farm, Alex Duarte, O.D., Ph.D., Brian Clement of Hippocrates Health Institute, Anna Maria Clement of Hippocrates Health Institute, Don Christopher of Christopher Ranch, Dian Dincin Buchman, Ph.D., Eric Block, Ph.D., Bill Anderson of Garlic Research Labs, Gary Abrams, M.D., Chester J. Cavalito, Ph.D., Angela M. O'Callaghan, C.J. Scheiner, M.D., Ph.D.
- New York Public Library
- Tim and Nina Zagat for their super ZAGAT SURVEYS
- Rudy Shur and Avery Publishing Group for healthful recipes
- Lawrence P. Ashmead, a great and thoughtful friend
- Don Hauptman for opening his files to us and always sharing

- Alyce Finell for words and music to "The Garlic Song"
- Those who generously contributed to our quest for everything garlic: Diane and Irv Wilen, Robert Weinstein, Marion Weber, Judy Twersky, Elliot Tiber, Mauri Small, Mae Schenk, Nancy Rajala, Buddy Radisch, Betsy Pryor, Robert Pardi, B.L. Ochman, Eileen Nock, Blanche Miller, Brenda Miao, Jokasha Klest, Hans Klein, Bob Kinkead, Arlen Hollis Kane, Martha Holmberg, George Hartman, Lewis Harrison, Gayle Gardner, Helen Burgess, Ihsan Aziz, Dr. Lou Arone, Sheila Anderson, John Amorosso, Mike Weiss and PCSI
- And special thanks to Linda Wilen, whose computer saved the day. They say, "You can choose your friends, not your relatives." What a bonus to have a relative we choose as a friend!

Introduction

French philosopher Blaise Pascal said, "The last thing we decide in writing a book is what to put first." And so it is with this introduction—the last of the pages yet to be written before handing in our manuscript. Now that the rest of the book has been completed, well, almost, we look back . . .

We knew that garlic was an effective ingredient used for many ailments—our folk remedy books attest to that—but we had no idea how very beneficial it is. We soon discovered that there are over 2,000 published papers on recent research documenting garlic's health-promoting properties, and there are many more promising studies being conducted currently.

Before working on this book, neither of us ever ate raw garlic. Now we don't stop. One of the reasons that this book took so long was that we experimented until we found ways to safely, and painlessly, eat raw garlic while keeping our breath kissing sweet.

We also interviewed dozens of health professionals—doctors who practice conventional medicine, as well as others with alternative and complementary practices—and all of them, without exception, eat garlic and recommend it to most of their patients.

There's even a Dracula/garlic connection. Wait till you read the real story behind, "I vant to darink your blahd."

No Matter How You Say It . . . Garlic in 45 Languages

The Word *garlic* comes from the Anglo-Saxon *garleac*, meaning "spear-leek." Garlic was known as the spear plant because of its flat, pointed, spearlike leaves.

In ancient Greece, it was called *scorodon*, thought to be derived from *skaion rodon* and said to mean *rose puante*, or "stinking rose."

The Latin and botanical name for garlic is *Allium sativum*, a member of the lily family whose siblings are other *Alliums:* onions, leeks, chives, scallions, and shallots. The word *Allium* may be derived from the Latin *olere*, "to smell," or the Greek *hallesthai*, describing the "springing up" stem, or from the Celtic *all-brennend*, "sharp taste, burning." *Sativum* means "cultivated." Garlic has, indeed, been cultivated since before recorded history. As a writer and faculty member at the Rocky Mountain Center for Botanical Studies in Colorado so eloquently put it, "A measure of humanity's love for this herb is that it has spread in this cultivated form to every continent capable of growing it, with the bulbs planted by hand generation after generation since prehistory."

For those with an insatiable *Allium sativum* appetite, carry this list with you when you travel abroad and see how the appropriate magic word will pop out at you on menus. And if it's not there, you'll now know how to order it. (The spelling may vary within each country.)

Albanian	hudhrë
Anglo-Saxon	garleac
Arabian	thum, tsoum
Babylonian	ha-za-nu
Basque	berakatz
Chinese	da suan
Czechoslovakian	česnek

4

Danish	hvidløg
Dutch	knoflook
Esperanto	ajlo
Estonian	küüskauk
Finnish	valkosipuli, laukka
French	ail
German	Knoblauch
Greek	skor'don
Haitian	Lai
Hawaiian	'Aka'Akai-Pilau
Hebrew	schum
Hindi	lashun
Hungarian	fokhagyma
Icelandic	knapplaukur
Indonesian	bawang putih
Italian	aglio, agliotti, ai
Japanese	ninniku
Latin, ancient	scordium, theriaca rusticorum
Latin, scientific	Allium sativum
Latvian	kiploki
Lithuanian	chesnakas
Maltese	tewm
Norwegian	hvitløk
Polish	czosnek
Portuguese	alho
Rumanian	usturoi
Russian	chesnók
Sanskrit	aristha, lashuna
Serbo-Croatian	beli luk
South African	knoffel
Spanish	ajo

Swahili	kitunguu saumu
Swedish	vitlök
Swiss	chnoble
Tamil	irulli
Turkish	sarmisak
Welsh	garlleg
Yiddish	knobel

"Garlic's Believe It or Not"

HISTORIC FACTS, TRADITIONS, FOLK LEGENDS, AND WHAT HAVE YOU

My Kind of Town—Cigaga-Wunji Is

"The Spanish conquistadores introduced the Stinking Lily (garlic) to the New World; proof of its popularity is the name *Chicago*, derived from the Native American name *Cigaga-Wunji*, or 'place of garlic,' " says Rita Aero in *The Complete Book of Longevity*.

We could let it go at that, but in all fairness to historian Irving Cutler, author of *Chicago—Metropolis of the Mid Continent*, we need to mention that he believes the name of his "toddling town" came from the Native American *Che Ca Gou* which means "strong-smelling wild onions of the mud flats." They're probably both right—it just depends on which Native American nation you talk to.

It's Greek to Me

In Homer's *Odyssey*, the Greek epic poet had Ulysses use garlic as a source of strength against Circe the sorceress.

Folk Legend

Scandinavian shepherds are said to rub their hands with blessed garlic before milking their animals. To protect the herd from trolls, a few garlic cloves are hung around each animal's neck.

And Yet Another Use for Garlic

An Asian healing modality is *moxibustion*, a form of acupuncture using heat instead of needles. An Asian practitioner places *moxas*—little cones of mugwort powder—over acupuncture points on the skin, and then they're ignited. They smolder slowly, similar to incense. A thin slice of garlic runs interference between the skin and the moxa cone, to prevent the skin from overheating and scarring.

9

"Out of This World" Super Syrup

This was reprinted in *The Inner Voice*, a Wisconsin publication that reprinted it from *Harmonic Response Messenger*, a Washington publication for which we could not find a listing. Nor could we find Lavinia Ritkiss, a healer in Los Angeles, who was supposedly given the Space Syrup as a gift from aliens to humankind. Even though we are unable to confirm this story in any way, we are including it for your amusement and/or good health.

Seven small green creatures appeared out of thin air in the corner of her office. "They seemed very loving and concerned," the California health guru recalled. "They told me they had a great affection and respect for humans and wanted to help us with this gift.

"It contains many ingredients that humans use to improve health, but the formula the aliens' advanced science has produced combines these ingredients in a new and different way, and it has a remarkable impact on the body."

Mrs. Ritkiss says, "The aliens told me that it affects the electrical energy of the body, reversing negative impulses that bring about diseases and unhealthy emotions."

The day after the visitation, Mrs. Ritkiss mixed up a batch of the syrup. Because it contained nothing she felt would harm her, she took a teaspoon every day for a month to see what would happen.

"My arthritis is gone, my skin glows, even my teeth and hair are different. I feel like a teenager again," says the recipe recipient. "Since then, I have shared the recipe with hundreds of people, and it has cured everything—acne, heart disease, depression, and even cancer. The syrup is so wonderful, I know I have to tell everybody about it. It's a miracle gift, a token of love from outer space," declared Lavinia Ritkiss.

SPACE SYRUP

Ingredients:
2 teaspoons diced fresh garlic
3 tablespoons olive oil
5 tablespoons pure clover honey
1 tablespoon apple cider vinegar
1/2 teaspoon cayenne pepper

optional: 1/4 teaspoon asafoetida
1/4 cup strong green tea, freshly made

Sauté garlic in olive oil for 1 minute, then add other ingredients. Simmer and cook over low flame for 5 minutes. Let cool. Strain into a glass jar. Cover and refrigerate. Take 1 teaspoon a day.

Baby Breath

Hippocrates used garlic to determine the child-bearing potential of a woman. A peeled clove of garlic was placed in the woman's vagina and left there overnight. Next morning, if the smell of garlic was on her breath, she was deemed capable of conceiving a child.

Incidentally, Hippocrates, called the Father of Medicine, considered garlic one of the most important of his 400 therapeutic remedies and used it to treat infections, wounds, digestive problems, cancer, and leprosy.

Get Out the E-Z-Rol

Ayurvedic practitioners in India used garlic to treat leprosy. When India became a member of the British Commonwealth of Nations, they adopted English, and leprosy became known as *peelgarlic* because the lepers spent so much time peeling garlic to eat as part of their treatment.

Folk Legend

Greek midwives decorated birthing rooms with cloves of garlic to safeguard newborn babes from disease, demons, witches, evil spirits, as well as snakes, which are repelled by the smell.

This Could Be the Start of Something Big

Garlic, dating back to 3000 B.C., is one of the oldest cultivated plants. It's thought to be native to Central Asia, where it grows wild. Speculation on how it became cultivated also grows wild.

Legend has it that Emperor Huang-ti of Hsia or Xia, the first Chinese dynasty (traditionally dated c. 2205–1766 B.C.), journeyed up a mountain with his followers. Along the way, the followers ate plant leaves that proved to be poisonous, and they became deathly ill. Fortunately, wild garlic was also growing there. They ate the garlic, and their lives were saved. That dramatic incident prompted Emperor Huang-ti to introduce the bulb into cultivation.

Say It With Flowers . . . or Not

In the early nineteenth century, the custom in certain circles was to communicate through the language of flowers. For instance, if a man sent a woman white lilies, according to G. W. Gessmann's guide *Blumensprache*, he was telling her: "You are as innocent as this symbol of innocence."

Garlic blossoms, though a member of the lily family, conveyed a message you wouldn't want to get: "What I feel for you is the utmost indifference."

Natural Magic

Draja Mickaharic, author of *A Century of Spells*, explains how garlic can be used in baths for personal protection.

> *"Boil 9 cloves of garlic in an iron (or stainless steel) pot with about a quart of water. Boil for about 20 minutes, allow the solution to cool to room temperature. Take a regular cleansing bath, with soap and water, then pour the garlic solution over your head, allowing it to flow away down the bath drain while praying that evil be washed off. This bath is effective against most negative influences, particularly against the physical debilitation brought on by the evil eye or consistent negativity from others."*

Speaking of the evil eye . . . According to Draja, carrying around three garlic cloves in a red charm bag helps ward off the evil eye.

Open Wide and Say G-AHHHHH-RLIC

Physician and Nobel Peace Prize winner Dr. Albert Schweitzer, who founded a missionary hospital in Africa (present-day Gabon), used garlic in treating cholera, typhus, and typhoid.

Sign of the Times

Bumper sticker from the first Gilroy Garlic Festival in 1979: "Fight Mouthwash, Eat Garlic."

What's Cooking?

The Norman Crusaders are credited with introducing to England an interest in food in the eleventh century. Instead of the boiled dishes and cabbage of the Saxons, the Normans preferred goose cooked with garlic and chicken with cumin.

The Chinese have been cooking with garlic for over 4,000 years, now averaging five cooked garlic cloves a day per person.

Alliumaniacs

Ancient Egyptians were crazy about garlic! When taking solemn oaths, they swore on garlic, just as we swear on the Bible.

According to hieroglyphic records, laborers building the pyramids of Cheops were given daily doses of garlic to help keep them healthy and maintain their strength and stamina. It is said that a strong male slave could be bought for 15 pounds of garlic.

In 1922, when King Tutankhamen's tomb was found and opened, among all the priceless treasures placed there around 1400 B.C. were six dried and perfectly preserved garlic bulbs.

A Clove Affair

Author of *The Supermarket Sorceress*, high priestess Lexa Roséan suggests a sure-fire way to heat up a lustless relationship. Roast 2 bulbs of garlic (see Recipes chapter if you need instructions).

Once the bulbs are cool enough to touch, each of you select one and squish out your own initial on a slice of bread, then feed it to the other. All you need is love . . . and garlic.

Folk Legend

Everyone knows that you repel a vampire with garlic. But do you know how the legend came to be? Dr. James Scala explains, "Porphyria is a hereditary disease that occurred in isolated areas of central Europe, especially Rumania, where Transylvania is located. People with porphyria need iron in the form of hemoglobin from blood. They must avoid sunlight or any strong indoor light or their skin becomes inflamed and produces toxins that make them very sick. They are exceptionally hairy, have large teeth, and very light skin. Most importantly, diallyl sulfides make them violently ill. Garlic is the best source of diallyl sulfides. Therefore, whoever has hereditary porphyria looks and acts like a vampire and will avoid garlic like the plague." Which brings us to—

Plague Potion

Marseilles, 1721, during an outbreak of bubonic plague:

Version #1: Four convicted criminals were assigned to bury those who had succumbed to the dreaded disease. Since whoever came in contact with the virulent plague-causing bacteria contracted the disease and died in three days, it was thought to be a death sentence for the four grave-diggers. But nooooooo! They were immune to it because they drank and doused their faces and clothes with a mixture of garlic and other herbs in wine or vinegar. Government officials offered the men amnesty in exchange for their secret formula, which came to be known as "Four Thieves Vinegar."

Version #2: A man named Richard Forthave developed a preparation that provided complete protection against the plague. It was referred to as "Forthave's," Richard's surname. Through the years, as the story was passed from generation to generation, the name changed from "Forthave's" to "Four Thieves."

This is the "Four Thieves Vinegar" (*Vinaigre des Quatres Voleurs*) recipe that was said to have been used in Marseilles:

Version #1: Crush 50 cloves of garlic and add it to 3 pints of white wine vinegar, along with a handful each of wormwood, wild marjoram, sage, meadowsweet, rosemary, and horehound, then add 2 ounces each of campanula roots and angelica, plus a 3-pound measure of camphor.

Version #2: Add 1/4 ounce each of calamus root, cinnamon, ground nutmeg, lavender, mint, rosemary, rue, sage, and wormwood, and 2 minced garlic bulbs to 2 pints cider vinegar. Cover and keep warm for 5 days. Strain and add 1/4 ounce powdered camphor before bottling.

If you visit France, don't be surprised to see "Four Thieves Vinegar" as a commercially bottled product.

Throwing the Bull

Bolivian bullfighters of the Aymara Indians carry a clove of garlic with them into the ring. The thinking is, if the bull smells the garlic, he will not charge.

Going for the Garlic and the Gold

In ancient Greece, for added energy and endurance, Olympic athletes ate garlic before competing.

The Greek folk name for the pungent herb was *thériaké, meaning "poor-man's treacle" (antidote).*

Words to Live By

Motto of the Washington, D.C., annual Garlic Festival: "It's Chic to Reek."

Gimme That Old Time Religion

The Talmud, compilations of the Oral Law of the Jews, mentions garlic many times for various reasons: keeping the body warm, brightening up the face, killing parasites in the body, removing jealousy, and the recommendation that it be eaten on the eve of the Sabbath, to assure the sanctioned Friday night love-making by married couples.

The Zodiac Connection

Garlic's corresponding planetary ruler is Mars, and its astrological influences are Aries and Scorpio.

Folk Legend

Garlic—a bulb, bunches of bulbs, braided bulbs, or a garlic wreath, in a variety of places—hanging over the door, fastened to a doorpost, or on a mantel is said to do a range of good things, from keeping evil spirits away to bringing good luck and prosperity.

Hanging garlic in the kitchen should absorb negative energy and prevent accidents and food poisoning.

Garlic hung over a marital bed ensures that the couple will have children.

Folk Legend

Garlic cooked on Saint John's Eve (June 23) and eaten the following day is thought to protect against malevolent influences throughout the year. In the Italian community, the belief is that it will prevent poverty.

Sleep . . . Perchance to Dream

Migene Gonzalez-Wippler says in *Dreams and What They Mean to You*, "This gives the traditional or fixed meaning for each dream motif. The personal conditions of the dreamer and his or her immediate environment must also be taken into consideration." And so it is with all the following dream interpretations:

Dream of garlic and you will rise from poverty to prosperity and wealth. Numbers 22 and 36 are ascribed to the dream by popular tradition and are believed to be lucky in games of chance.

In *Dreams—Hidden Meanings and Secrets* by Orion, to dream of smelling garlic foretells some achievement that will bring you recognition in the field of sports.

If, in your dream, you use garlic as a seasoning, you will receive a letter that for a time will give you much concern.

The Complete Dream Book by Edward Frank Allen states that an improvement in both your financial and love affairs is presaged by a dream of walking through a garlic patch.

A young woman who dreams of eating garlic will make a marriage based on money considerations rather than love.

Gustavus Hindman Miller in his *10,000 Dreams Interpreted* says that eating garlic in your dreams denotes that you will take a sensible view of life and leave its ideals to take care of themselves.

The take on dreaming of garlic in *The Dreamers Dictionary* by Lody Stearn Robinson and Tom Corbett is that it's considered an omen of general welfare and protection, unless you are one of the people who loathe it, in which case it must be considered a sign of some brief but annoying unpleasantness.

Zolar's Encyclopedia & Dictionary of Dreams declares that when you dream of garlic, you will discover a secret:

- Eating garlic: You will have a big quarrel.
- Buying garlic: You will be irritated by other people.
- Cooking with garlic: You are disliked by those working under you.
- Growing garlic in a garden: People detest you.
- Giving children garlic to eat: They will realize high position.
- Dream of people who don't like garlic: They are unfit to fill your position.

Therein Lies the Rub

Master herbalist Maurice Messegue, who believed garlic to be synonymous with vitality, talks about a French tradition, "In Gascony we say that we baptize our children by rubbing a clove of garlic on their tongues and following that up with a swallow of Armagnac [a dry brandy]. Then they are ready to meet whatever challenges life brings."

Folk Legend

In parts of the Middle East, tradition has it that if a clove of garlic is worn by a bridegroom on his wedding garment, he will have a blissful wedding night.

The Braidy Bunch

At harvest time on the Christopher Ranch near Gilroy, California, a group of itinerant workers gather to braid specially grown garlic. Each braid contains 19 to 21 bulbs, weighs about 3 pounds, and is 2 feet long. A fast braider can produce 130 units a day.

Playing Catch-Up

The Codex Ebers, an Egyptian medical papyrus dating back to about 1550 B.C., gives 22 uses for garlic, including headaches, worms, bites, heart problems, and tumors. Now, some 3,500 years later, scientific researchers are coming to the same conclusion.

Garlic, the Aphrodisiac

"Garlic is a natural, safe, and effective aphrodisiac," says C.J. Scheiner, M.D., PhD., and foremost authority on erotica. "Garlic contains various chemicals that are both fat soluble and water soluble. They will get into the components of the genital-urotal tract and will cause a mild irritation that produces a very pleasant effect." Dr. Scheiner explains that it works in the same way that the canthracides do in Spanish fly, but to a much lesser degree, and without the potentially-fatal side effects

"The amount of garlic needed for this purpose varies with each person," according to Dr. Scheiner. "One clove may be enough for some; ten cloves not enough for others.

"Italian men have the reputation of always being sexually excited. Perhaps it's due to the large amount of garlic in their daily diet. They may be in a constant state of genital-urotal irritation."

Garlic
as Medicine

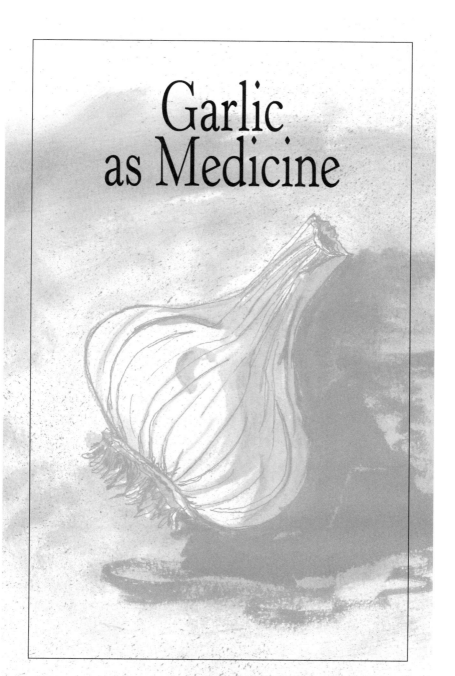

Garlic . . .
The flower of life . . .
The repellent of vampires . . .
The clove of health . . .
The bulb of bad breath . . .
The drug of choice . . .

Gloria Morrison

Powdered garlic (bought in bulk at an herb store) or Lalitha's Enhanced Garlic Formula (in Preparations chapter under Nature's Amazing Antibiotic) can be applied topically as a dusting powder for infection, fungus, rash, or mild skin abrasions.

Used as a poultice, the powder is moistened with a little water, aloe vera gel, honey (not for outdoor animals, as honey draws insects), or other moistening agent and applied 1/8 to 1/2 inch thick to the affected area. Clean the affected part with garlic water, or other disinfecting wash, and repack with a fresh poultice two to five times a day, depending upon the seriousness of the condition.

Chopped, crushed, or sliced fresh garlic can be used alone or mixed with another of Lalitha's selected herbs—chaparral, comfrey, slippery elm, yarrow—as a poultice 1/8 to 1/2 inch thick over the area. For a small need, such as a scratch or insect bite, tape a slice of garlic, juicy side down, onto the area. These poultices will speed healing and prevent or treat infection.

Raw garlic juice can be rubbed onto an affected body part. Simply cut a clove of garlic and rub the juicy part onto the area.

Scientists seem to agree that garlic is extremely—even exceptionally—helpful in preventing, improving, and curing many ailments.

As for dosage, we report suggested dosages when they were reported to us. Naturally, you must take into consideration your size, age, condition, and your garlic tolerance level. You may need to start slowly and work your way up to the reported dose. If raw garlic is suggested and you absolutely cannot take it, then use supplements (capsules, pills, pearles/soft gels), juice, soup, tonics, oil, baths, enemas, suppositories—whatever form seems to work best for you and is most appropriate for the condition.

We urge you to check with your health professional before starting any self-help treatment.

Renowned herbalist Lalitha Thomas has given us permission to reprint dosage information from her excellent book *Ten Essential Herbs* (Hohm Press). Garlic, of course, is included among her chosen ten.

GENERAL DOSAGE: INTERNAL USE

Adults:

- Garlic oil, 1 or 2 teaspoons, as often as every 2 hours up to eight times a day, depending upon the seriousness of the condition.
- Or, powdered garlic (bought in bulk at an herb store), 1/4 to 1/2 teaspoon, as often as every 2 hours up to eight times a day, depending upon the seriousness of the condition.
- Or, powdered garlic in the form of Lalitha's Special Enhanced Formula (in the Preparations chapter under Nature's Amazing Antibiotic), 1/2 to 1 teaspoon, as often as every 2 hours up to eight times a day, depending upon the seriousness of the condition.
- Or, fresh raw garlic (average size 1 inch long by 1/2 inch wide), 1 or 2 cloves, eaten as often as every 2 hours up to five times a day, depending upon the seriousness of the condition.

In mild cases of cold or flu, congestion, cough, and so on, generally three to four doses are all that is needed during a day. (See *Seven Easy Ways to Eat Raw Garlic*.)

GENERAL DOSAGE: EXTERNAL USE

Use garlic externally as an antibiotic, insect repellent, fungicide, or against parasites.

Garlic oil can be rubbed into the affected body part, or if an infection is in the ear, the oil can be used as eardrops.

*Our apothecary's shop is our garden full of pot herbs,
and our doctor is a good clove of Garlic.*

Poet Unknown
A Deep Snow, 1615

WHAT TO TAKE, HOW, AND WHY

If you are planning to add garlic to your daily diet and/or to your regimen of supplements, you should know some basic information about this magnificently complex vegetable.

William Blot, chief biostatistician of the National Cancer Institute, explains, "Every time you slice or crush a clove of garlic, you initiate a complex sequence of biochemical events. The merest bruise unleashes an enzyme called allinase, which goes to work converting another molecule, alliin, into allicin. That this reaction is instantaneous is obvious because at precisely this moment, garlic begins to smell like garlic.

"Allicin spontaneously decomposes into a group of odoriferous compounds which provide much of garlic's medicinal punch. Those compounds quickly form still others—dozens of them—depending on whether the bulb is fresh or aged, raw or cooked, natural or processed in pills, extracts, and capsules.

"Garlic's quicksilver nature creates problems for researchers. No one really knows which form delivers the greatest benefit."

Aha! *No one really knows which form delivers the greatest benefit.*

To recap, once a garlic clove is bruised in any way (cut, crushed, mashed, pressed, diced, sliced, minced), through a highly intricate conversion process, allicin is formed.

Allicin is the sulfur compound that has caused the "with it" or "without it" controversy among supplement manufacturers.

We have done extensive research on the extensive research that has been done with regard to the medicinal efficacy of garlic. The only thing that's conclusive is that nothing is conclusive, except that most of the doctors and research scientists we interviewed agreed that raw garlic has the best antibiotic effects.

If you don't have a physical problem for which garlic may be harmful, but you have not been able to eat raw garlic simply because it's too strong, see helpful hints below.

THE SECRET OF SELECTING THE BEST SUPPLEMENTS

Commercial supplements should not be chosen by impressive advertising campaigns, and high-priced pills do not mean they're better. There are many supplements on the market. In one vitamin store catalogue, we counted 25 different garlic supplements ranging from allicin-free (odorless) aged garlic extract capsules, to time-release allicin-rich (odorless) caplets, to allicin-rich (odorous) pills.

Varro E. Tyler, professor of pharmnocognosy (drugs from natural sources) at Purdue University, told us that *enteric coated* garlic supplements are recommended for maximum absorption of allicin. A supplement that is enteric coated resists the effects of stomach acid and allows the intestinal enzymes to dissolve it so that the full benefit of the supplement is derived. Check labels for the words "enteric coated."

Garlic oil—in the form of pearles or soft gels—is made of compounds that are derived only from allicin. Research scientist Larry D. Lawson explains that the steam-distilling process that converts and extracts the oil is too strong to use, so it's always greatly diluted with something like soybean oil. You may want to check the label for the ingredient in which the garlic oil is suspended.

"Basically, it's a consumer-beware market for garlic supplements," says Elizabeth Somer, M.A., R.D. "Some garlic products have 33 times more of certain compounds than other garlic products. Unless the label lists specific amounts (per capsule or tablet) of active ingredients, such as allicin, S-allyl-cysteine, ajoene, diallyl sulfides, or at least total sulfur content, then assume the product is 'condiment grade' and no better, or worse, than garlic powder seasoning, which seems to be a perfectly viable source of most garlic constituents."

GENERAL TIPS

- Most companies have toll-free numbers on their labels. If you have questions, call and ask them about their product.

- Raw, finely chopped garlic contains significant amounts of allicin and is thought to be the most effective form of garlic for use as an antibiotic.

- If you are working on a health challenge and garlic is part of your treatment, to assure maximum effectiveness, take doses throughout the day. This does not mean *increasing* the amount of garlic that's appropriate for the problem, it just means don't take the daily dosage at one time . . . space it out.

- Taking 2 or 3 fresh garlic cloves will equal 4 (1,000 mg) powdered garlic tablets or 1 teaspoon garlic powder (the supermarket stuff).

- Dr. Larry Lawson, respected garlic researcher, says you should eat raw garlic after you've had a few mouthfuls of food or right after a meal. Eating garlic on an empty stomach may cause irritation and discomfort.

SEVEN EASY WAYS TO EAT RAW GARLIC

As authors of this garlic book, we thought eating garlic is something we should do, but neither of us could tolerate it raw. We followed our own advice from our folk remedy books: finely mince a clove of garlic, put it in orange juice or water, and drink it down. That worked with one little clove, but anything larger than that would cause each of us to double over in pain—excruciating burning pain as the garlic made its way down.

The more we learned about the benefits of garlic, the more we wanted to eat garlic, and the more garlic we wanted to eat. So we started experimenting. By far, the best, most delicious and soothing way for us to eat raw garlic is in a dollop of plain, nonfat yogurt. This method has also helped us build a tolerance for it, and we're now having raw garlic in salads and adding it to dishes *after* they've been cooked.

Minced garlic in a tablespoon of honey also makes it easy to take, if you don't mind the sweetness. (The combination of honey and garlic is also a good cough medicine.)

Ronald Hoffman, M.D., shares his method:

"I find that a convenient way to mask the taste of garlic, when I want to eat it raw, is to take a bite of the clove and then take a bite of a kosher dill pickle which is already in garlic. What I get is a super garlic pickle taste that's tolerable." Dr. Hoffman is quick to caution, "Of course it's not for people who're watching their salt intake."

When asked about eating pickled garlic, Dr. Hoffman says he thinks it's good and can't imagine that the pickling process would take away from the benefits.

Miso is a thick fermented paste made with soybeans, rice, or barley (available at health food stores and Asian groceries). Garlic pickled in miso will mellow its pungency, making it easy to take.

To prepare miso-pickled garlic, fill a small wide-mouth glass jar with miso. Slice peeled garlic cloves in half lengthwise and push them into the miso—as many as will fit, making sure that each half clove is surrounded by miso. Close the jar tightly and refrigerate for a month. Then eat the cloves at your own pace. (Rinse off the miso before eating each half-clove.) It's best to finish all the cloves within a month or two, before their alliin content diminishes. You can then use the garlicky miso as a tasty soup stock.

Garlic—juiced and whole cloves—along with wheatgrass therapy are part of the *living foods* program that has brought about miraculous healings at Hippocrates Health Institute in West Palm Beach, Florida.

According to co-director Anna Maria Clement, their method for eating raw garlic is to put a tablespoon of flaxseed in a glass of water and leave it overnight. In the morning, you will have a mucilaginous drink that will protect your stomach when eating raw garlic. Stir it, drink it, then eat one or two garlic cloves.

Hippocrates director Brian Clement says to take a big bite of apple (organic, of course) and chew it thoroughly, letting the apple's pectin get around your mouth before swallowing. Then pop a raw garlic clove. There shouldn't be any burning, even when it goes down, thanks to the enzymes and pectin in the apple.

Minced garlic in applesauce is also a tasty, painless way to eat raw garlic.

Warning

Do not eat garlic or take garlic supplements if you have a bleeding disorder, or ulcers, or are taking anticoagulants.

Caution

Too much raw garlic can cause headaches, diarrhea, gas, fever, and in extreme cases, gastric bleeding.

Good Advice

Whatever method you use to eat raw garlic, or whichever supplements you take, pay attention to your physical reaction to it. Your body will tell you all you need to know. You've just got to listen.

The ideal, of course, is to work with a health professional—someone whose medical practice is in keeping with your philosophical and physical approach to good health.

Above all, use intuitive common sense when it comes to your own body and well-being.

Remedies

AIDS . . . Strengthening the Immune System

A medical student working with Dr. Benjamin Lau, professor at California's Loma Linda University School of Medicine, found that human immunodeficiency virus (HIV), or the AIDS virus, did not grow well in the presence of garlic in tissue culture. "The possibilities seem staggering!" says Dr. Lau.

Many studies have been conducted using garlic as a treatment for AIDS. In one study, during a three-month period of AIDS patients taking only one clove of garlic daily, there were significant increases in their immune functions usually destroyed by the disease. In that and similar studies, AIDS symptoms—genital herpes, chronic diarrhea, candidiasis, and pansinusitis with recurrent fever—improved or cleared up completely.

The encouraging data suggest that further studies of garlic preparations as a combined immune enhancer and antimicrobial, especially, antiviral agent are warranted and are happening.

ALLERGIES . . . Garlic to the Rescue!

"As an antitoxin, garlic defends and strengthens the body against allergens," said Carlson Wade, one of the nation's foremost medical research reporters. "Garlic also prevents the release of histamine and other symptom-producing substances into respiratory tract tissues. It has other nutritionally therapeutic advantages as well in that it has neither stimulative or sedative side effects."

CARLSON WADE'S ALLERGY-EASE TONIC

Into 2 cups of freshly boiled water, add 3 crushed garlic cloves and 1 teaspoon grated ginger root. Cover pot with a tight lid and let it simmer for about 2 minutes. Remove from heat and place on heat-resistant and nonburning surface. Lift pot lid very, very carefully and not too closely (you do not want to burn yourself), deeply inhale the steam for about 3 minutes.

The allicin substance in the garlic will combine with the pungent odor of the ginger root to help open up blocked respiratory channels. Within minutes, the garlic will create a decongestant reaction so that you can breathe easier and better.

You can also fill a mug with the same brew. Add a squeeze of lemon or lime. A teaspoon of honey is optional. Sip while comfortably hot. This tangy Allergy-Ease Tonic will act as a potent decongestant. It will help you to relax and will also strengthen your resistance to allergic unrest.

Complementary medicine specialist Fred Pescatore, M.D., noticed that because of a tough winter, a larger-than-usual number of people came to him with allergy symptoms. People who had not had problems for years were troubled with sore throat, runny nose, itchy eyes—symptoms typical of sinus-type seasonal allergies.

We prescribe an allergy formula that, along with different ingredients like quercetin and citrus bioflavonoids, also has garlic in it. This year I've given my allergy patients an additional supplement of garlic in capsule form—about 400 mg, three times a day. My patients called to tell me how much better they felt. Or, when they came back two weeks later, they walked into my office symptom-free.

The garlic not only works as a decongestant, but it seems to enhance the effectiveness of other supplements that are given to help clear up the problem.

The doctor advises his patients to take garlic *before* the allergy seasons begin. It may help eliminate or lessen symptoms. It's also a good idea because it will presensitize one's system, so that if and when allergies are particularly bad, the presensitized person will be able to double the garlic dosage if needed. (Also see SINUS.)

ANEMIA . . . Nature's Blood Builder

Rex Adams, research reporter in the field of natural and drugless medicine, explains:

Anemia means that the body does not produce enough hemoglobin—the red oxygen-carrying substance in the blood. Hemoglobin can't be produced without iron. Along with an iron deficiency, anemia can result from inadequate protein, iodine, cobalt, copper, vitamin C, or any of the B vitamins. You may say that there aren't enough of any of these in garlic to affect most forms of anemia. However, there are these unique factors which may make garlic useful in such cases:

- It isn't enough to eat iron-rich foods or take iron supplements. It doesn't work unless there are enough B complex vitamins for the iron to be utilized. Garlic increases the absorption of B vitamins, especially vitamin B-1.
- Copper is needed for iron assimilation. Garlic contains traces of copper, which is a trace mineral needed only in minute quantities by the human body. Yet microscopic shortages can cause problems.
- Also important, copper is needed for the absorption and use of vitamin C from other foods. Vitamin C vastly increases the assimilation of iron from food.

If you take this information into consideration, you can clearly see the value of eating a couple of garlic cloves a day to help prevent anemia. (Also see BLOOD.)

ANIMAL BITES . . . First-Aid Kit in a Bulb

In an emergency, until you can get professional help:
According to herbalist Lalitha Thomas, author of *Ten Essential Herbs* (Hohm Press):

These wounds need to be cleaned at once with a strong antibiotic wash such as garlic water (see Preparations chapter) or a strong infusion of yarrow. Sometimes a bite that is mostly a series of puncture wounds, without much torn skin, needs to be soaked thoroughly in the antibiotic solution to deeply treat the punctures. Depending on the seriousness of the bite, it can then be wrapped with a garlic poultice (see Preparations chapter).

To stop bleeding that may accompany an animal bite, sprinkle cayenne pepper on the wound. It will sting; it will also stop the bleeding.

It's also a great idea to drink cayenne pepper—1/8 to 1/2 teaspoon in 1/2 glass of water or juice—to help combat mental and physical shock.

ARTERIOSCLEROSIS AND ATHEROSCLEROSIS . . . Nature's Own Blood Thinner

Arteriosclerosis is specifically related to the buildup of calcium deposits that causes thickening and hardening of the arteries and loss of elasticity. Atherosclerosis is a condition brought on by the buildup of fatty deposits on the inside artery walls. (Also see CHOLESTEROL.) Both of these conditions can cause hypertension, strokes, and angina.

To help prevent atherosclerosis, simply avoid animal fats. If you do eat fatty meat and other greasy foods, be sure to have raw garlic and onion, too. Or take a couple of garlic/onion pills daily. Keep in mind, no matter how much garlic and onion you have, you still have to cut down on your animal fat intake significantly to help prevent atherosclerosis.

Ronald Hoffman, M.D., says, "If you have a heart problem, you can take a blood thinner, a blood pressure lowerer, and a cholesterol-lowering drug. What's unique about garlic as a cardiovascular agent is it incorporates all three modes of action. Garlic is the ultimate cardiovascular herb."

Garlic has been known to unplug arteries. It helps cleanse the system by collecting and casting out toxic wastes. It also helps restore elasticity to the arteries. On a daily basis, eat a couple of raw garlic cloves or take garlic supplements (4 capsules, 500 mg each) throughout the day.

ARTHRITIS . . . Soothing Relief With Garlic

Garlic has been used to quiet arthritis pain fairly quickly. Rub the juicy side of a freshly cut clove of garlic on sore areas. If skin is sensitive, rub garlic oil (in Preparations chapter) on the skin. If you want a *hot* liniment with which to massage your aching joints, use Dian Dincin Buchman's formula (see Preparations chapter for the Anti-Infection Wash and Arthritis Pain Liniment).

Also, eat raw garlic or take several garlic supplements daily.

When the humidity takes its toll on your joints, drink Garlic Tea (see Preparations chapter) throughout the day. If you have the time and the place, put crushed garlic on the soles of your feet and sit with your feet up while sipping the tea.

Are you one of the few people who has access to fig leaves? In a glass, enamel, or porcelain pot, boil 10 fig leaves in a quart of water with a couple of garlic cloves for about 10 minutes. When it's cool enough to touch but still warm, strain out the leaves and the cloves. Drench a towel in the liquid, wring it out, and massage the painful arthritic area with the hot, wet towel. Keep redrenching, wringing, and massaging for 15 to 20 minutes.

ASTHMA . . . Breathe Freer and Easier

Dr. Fred Pescatore, complementary medicine specialist, has a patient whose 4-year-old daughter has asthma. The little girl was on conventional medication along with garlic pearles (soft gels). The mother thought that the garlic might be making her condition worse, so she stopped the garlic. After a dreadful winter and spring, the child's mother took her off the medication and started her back on garlic pearles. The mother recently reported, "My daughter's doing great!"

Dr. Pescatore says that a child's dose of garlic pearles is 100 milligrams three times a day. The doctor also urges parents to be sure their asthmatic child is closely monitored by a trusted health professional.

At the very first sign of an asthma attack, peel and finely mince a clove of garlic, add it to a tablespoon of raw honey, and swallow it. The combination of garlic and honey has been known to quell an attack.

We heard about a man who was able to ease off massive doses of cortisone by using garlic therapy. He started with one garlic clove a day. As he increased the number of garlic cloves he ate each day, his doctor decreased the amount of cortisone he was taking. After several months, he was eating 6 to 10 cloves of garlic a day, he was completely off cortisone, and he was not bothered by asthma.

It's unusual to find older Italians with asthma, tuberculosis, or gallbladder trouble. It may very well be because garlic and olive oil are used in 2 out of their 3 daily meals.

If you don't have a problem with sugar intake, here's an easy-to-prepare syrup from herbalist Mary Quelch:

EASY-TO-PREPARE SYRUP

Cover the bottom of a large soup bowl with a layer of thin garlic slices. Pour in enough maple syrup to completely cover the garlic slices. Let it stand for 5 hours. Pour the maple-garlic syrup into a glass jar, cover, and refrigerate. Take 1 teaspoon whenever you feel wheezy.

Incidentally, the leftover maple-marinated garlic slices are delicious to eat.

(See Preparations chapter for other Soothing Garlic Syrup recipes to keep on hand and take, 1 teaspoon at a time, when the wheezing starts. Also look for the Bronchitis and Asthma Tea recipe.)

ATHLETE'S FOOT (See FEET.)

BAD BREATH FROM GARLIC (See GARLIC BREATH.)

BLISTERS . . . Rub Away Discomfort

Medical research writer Rex Adams reported the story of a letter carrier who was in agony because of blisters on his feet from ill-fitting shoes. After unsuccessfully trying every pharmaceutical product on the market, he remembered the antiseptic properties of garlic and bought himself garlic pearles (soft gels). The postal employee punctured a couple of pearles, squeezed out the oil, and massaged it into his blistered feet. The next morning, the swelling was practically gone and there was no more pain. Neither snow now rain nor heat nor gloom of night nor blisters from ill-fitting shoes . . . (See the Foot Massage with Garlic Oil in Preparations chapter.)

BLOOD . . . And the Blood-Building Power of Garlic

Carlson Wade, highly respected medical reporter, explains,

> Garlic is known for having antihemolytic factors; name-ly, it is able to promote the increase of red cells and hemoglobin in the bloodstream and give your rivers of life a supercharging of vitality and energy.
>
> Garlic is also rich in allicin, a substance that is said to protect against bacterial infection and other blood disor-ders. Garlic also contains alliin (a sulfur-containing amino acid) which has an antibiotic effect to "knock out" and "defuse" the proliferation of potentially harm-ful wastes floating in your bloodstream. *No other food has this amazing blood-building power!*
>
> For a richer and healthier bloodstream, be sure to have several garlic cloves daily.

(See Preparations chapter for Carlson Wade's Iron Tonic to wake up your "tired blood." Also see ANEMIA.)

BLOOD CLOTS . . . For Prevention: Move Over Aspirin—Here's Garlic!

Garlic not only helps the body to break up clots, it also stops the platelets from sticking together, thus preventing the clotting from taking place. And there are many controlled studies to prove it.

According to English garlic researcher David Roser, just eat-ing one or two garlic cloves a day will go a long way in helping the blood-thinning, clot-preventing process.

Mahendra K. Jain, Ph.D., professor of biochemistry at the University of Delaware, states that one of garlic's most powerful and well-tested anticoagulant compounds is *ajoene*. Three ways to release the ajoene from garlic most effectively are:

- *Crush* garlic rather than chop it.
- Saute garlic lightly; cooking releases ajoene.
- Cook garlic with tomatoes or other acidic foods. A little acid releases ajoene.

Dr. Eric Block, professor of chemistry at the State University of New York at Albany, is credited with isolating the garlic chemical *ajoene*. He has said that garlic's anticoagulant activity is equal to or better than aspirin.

CAUTION: If you are taking blood-thinning medication, garlic may interfere with the drugs by making them more potent. Check with your health professional before adding garlic to your diet.

BLOOD PRESSURE . . . The Great Equalizer

Blood pressure is measured by two numbers: the first and higher number is the systolic, measuring the pressure inside the arteries the instant the heart beats; the second and lower number is the diastolic, measuring the pressure in the arteries when the heart is at rest.

Blood pressure that is considered "normal" is 120/80 or lower. If the higher (systolic) number is 140 or higher and/or the lower (diastolic) number is 90 or higher, you have high blood pressure (also referred to as "hypertension").

Garlic can help stabilize high blood pressure. But first, we would be very remiss if we didn't list the basic lifestyle adjustments important for lowering one's blood pressure:

- If you're overweight, diet sensibly.
- Cut down or cut out meat and other fatty foods.
- If you smoke, stop!
- If you drink alcohol and coffee, stop or keep it to a minimum.

- Reduce the stress in your life—meditate, try biofeedback, do yoga—find something simple and pleasant that's going to lower your stress level.
- Exercise daily.
- Eliminate salt from your diet—use garlic and kelp as salt substitutes, either by sprinkling the powders on food (exactly like salt) or adding minced garlic and crumbled kelp to salads and other dishes for which they're appropriate and flavorful.

Rex Adams, drugless medicine researcher explains:

Too much salt in the diet draws potassium out of the cells. Sodium (salt) enters, drawing in water, which is retained. Cells become waterlogged and the person feels bloated and appears overweight. That's where garlic and kelp come in. Of all vegetables, these are the richest sources of iodine for the thyroid. They are also rich in potassium, which pulls out salt and releases excess fluid.

(See Garlic Express in the Preparations chapter for subduing salt cravings.)

In 1948, Dr. F. G. Piotrowski of the University of Geneva announced his dramatic findings that garlic has a profound effect on bringing down high blood pressure.

The doctor discovered that garlic's sulfur compounds calm the nerves, strengthen the heart, and gently dilate congested and restricted blood vessels.

Take garlic daily—raw and cooked garlic is good, so are garlic supplements.

Start by taking garlic several times a day—2 to 5 raw cloves or 3 to 5 pearles four times a day. As your pressure gets lower, reduce the dosage. (See Buying a Home Blood Pressure Monitor, page 40.)

Varro E. Tyler, Ph.D., professor of pharmacology at Purdue University, recommends eating a few cloves of garlic daily, or taking "enteric coated" garlic capsules. Be sure "enteric coated" is printed on the label. That coating allows for maximum absorption of allicin, which is thought to be the ingredient in garlic that's responsible for lowering blood pressure. Follow the recommended dosage on the label.

According to health and nutrition researcher Lelord Kordel, "For some reason not exactly clear, garlic as a remedy for high blood pressure works much more effectively when combined with watercress, in tablet form (follow dosage on the label), and/or eat raw garlic and fresh watercress in salads."

Garlic can also help to rebalance low blood pressure problems. The same general principles for determining the dosage apply for low blood pressure as for high blood pressure.

Now, with the availability of affordable home blood pressure monitors, it's a good idea to monitor yourself. That doesn't mean taking your blood pressure every 5 minutes. In fact, allow days, even a week or two or three, for the garlic to kick in and start to make a difference.

Buying a Home Blood Pressure Monitor

Mechanical Blood Pressure Monitors are said to be the most accurate, but they take time, practice, and patience to master. Prices range from $15 to $20.

Electronic Monitors do not require a stethoscope and so they are the easiest to use. They are especially good for people with vision, hearing, or dexterity problems. Prices range from $20 to $200 (you can get a good one for under $100).

Finger Monitors are expensive and thought to be less accurate than the monitors that use the *arm* rather than the *finger*. The arm is closer to the heart, which may account for greater accuracy.

Note: Before shopping for a Blood Pressure Monitor, measure your upper arm. If it's larger than 13 inches, you will most likely have to order a monitor that has a larger arm cuff.

Once you own a home monitor, take it with you to your next doctor's visit. In the office, take your blood pressure with your machine, then have the doctor take your blood pressure with the office machine. If you both get the same reading, you'll know you're doing it correctly and that you can count on the accuracy of your home monitor.

BODY ODOR (from garlic) . . . Soak Away the Smell

Yes, the smell of garlic may come out of your pores and be offensive to those around you. There are two solutions: Hang out only with other garlic-eaters or take a hot bath. You may want to add a pleasant-smelling herb like lavender to the water for your own enjoyment as you soak in the tub for a relaxing 15 to 20 minutes. By the end of that time, most of the garlic scent should be washed away.

BREAST-FEEDING (nursing) . . . Whet Baby's Appetite

According to a study done at the Monell Chemical Senses Center in Pennsylvania, an infant's appetite for breast milk may be stimulated if the mother eats garlic an hour before she begins breast-feeding. The study showed that the garlic's strong flavor and odor encouraged infants to nurse longer and drink more.

BRONCHITIS . . .
Calm the Cough; Clear Up the Condition

When you have congestion in your chest, do not have dairy products. Those mucus-producing foods and drinks will add to the problem. Instead, eat fruits and vegetables. Also have chicken soup with lots of garlic in it, of course. Drink garlic tea throughout the day. Take garlic syrup when the cough starts acting up. (See COLDS/FLU in Remedies chapter for Dr. Ziment's Garlic Chicken Soup, and Preparations chapter for Bronchitis and Asthma Tea and Soothing Garlic Syrups.)

BURNS (minor ones only)

Run cold water over the burned area. Once the heat is out of it, puncture a garlic pearle (soft gel) and squeeze the oil directly on the affected spot.

If it's a serious burn—blisters, broken or blackened skin—oil is the worst thing to apply. It will seal in the heat. So, remember . . . this is for *minor* burns only.

CANCER . . . Prevention and Treatment: New Hope With Garlic

Sidney Belman, New York University Medical Center professor of environmental medicine, and Michael J. Wargovich, Ph.D., cell biologist at the University of Texas System Cancer Center in Houston, agree that serious garlic-eaters have a lower rate and risk of stomach and colon cancer.

Dr. Wargovich cites a study of Northern Italy where garlic and onions are not eaten to any extent and stomach cancer is prevalent, compared to the garlic- and onion-eaters in Southern Italy where there is much less incident of stomach cancer.

Dr. Wargovich, who studies the medicinal properties of natural foods, says, "It seems that chemicals in garlic and onions go to our liver and stimulate some of the enzymes that help detoxify hazardous chemicals in the environment which might include carcinogens (cancer-causing substances)."

Several research teams have seen that sulfides, the odor-causing substance in garlic, block the action of cancer-causing substances and also inhibit or slow down tumor development. Testing continues.

Meanwhile, the findings of studies conducted by Dr. Wang Meiling of the Shanong Medical Research Institute in Tianjin, China, indicate that cancer deaths in garlic-loving countries are almost ten times lower than elsewhere.

William Blot, chief biostatistician of the National Cancer Institute, says, "The weight of evidence is making it look like garlic really is protective against cancer."

Dr. John Pinto of the Memorial Sloan-Kettering Cancer Center in New York says, "There is growng evidence that garlic or its derivatives may be able to prevent the development of at least six different cancers—cancer of the breast, colon, esophagus, prostate, skin, and stomach."

Throughout the forty-year history of Hippocrates Health Institute (now in West Palm Beach, Florida), America's first and foremost *life-change center*, thousands of people believe that they have healed themselves of cancer with the use of the Institute's program of living foods, wheatgrass and garlic therapy.

Brian R. Clement, director of Hippocrates, states,

"Through our extensive use of garlic in our program, we are very clear that its natural chemical agents not only help boost and elevate the immune system to fight off and eliminate disease, but also help to strengthen the red blood cells of the body, which are the building blocks of all bone, cells, tissue, etc.

"The new buzzword when discussing nutrition and cancer is *phytochemicals*. Phytochemicals are components within natural food that have been proven to retard cancer development and growth. Garlic contains phytochemicals—allylic sulfides—which work by waking up enzymes that detoxify cancer-causing chemicals inside cells.

Clement, author of *Living Foods for Optimum Health*, says, "Of all foods, garlic is probably the number one natural healing agent."

CANDIDA ALBICANS (See YEAST INFECTION.)

CHOLESTEROL . . . Raise the Good (HDL); Lower the Bad (LDL)

In an effort to give you an understanding of cholesterol, here is a simplified explanation: Cholesterol is a soft, waxy substance found in our cells and bloodstream. It's vital for healthy cell function and hormone and vitamin D production.

Cholesterol makes its way through the bloodstream via special protein carriers called lipoproteins. The two main lipoproteins are low-density lipoproteins (LDLs) and high-density lipoproteins

(HDLs). The LDLs are the "bad" cholesterol; the HDLs are the "good" cholesterol.

The bad LDLs can form artery-clogging plaque (see ATHERO-SCLEROSIS); the good HDLs carry cholesterol away from the blood-stream, helping to prevent the development of atherosclerosis.

We get cholesterol from eating foods that come from ani-mals—that means meat, poultry, fish, seafood, dairy products, eggs, and products made from these foods.

Almost two dozen published tests on humans conclude that daily doses of fresh garlic and some garlic preparations help raise good HDL and lower bad LDL levels.

Robert I-San Lin, Ph.D., chairperson of an International Conference on Garlic as Medicine, says that three garlic cloves a day can lower cholesterol an average of 10 to 15 percent in some people. A 10 percent drop in cholesterol translates into a 20 per-cent drop in the risk of heart attack.

Cooked garlic and pickled garlic are also beneficial for help-ing to bring down cholesterol, as is extra virgin olive oil (in mod-eration, of course).

You may want to check out the Recipe section for dishes that combine olive oil and garlic.

Remember, lie low on the foods that are high in low-density lipoproteins . . . *animal* products.

COLDS/FLU . . .
Making Them Yesterday's News

The average American adult (without children) gets about two and a half colds annually. If that adult has children, he or she can expect more than that because young children, whose immune systems are less developed than adults', average eight to ten colds a year, and some of those colds are passed on to the parent(s).

Garlic seems to be the universal cold/flu remedy. Every coun-try has its own ways of using it. Select the one that's most appro-priate for you:

At the onset of a cold, peel 2 small cloves of garlic and keep them in your mouth, one on each side, between your cheek and your teeth; the cold will disappear within a few hours or, at most, within a day, according to Kristine Nolfi, M.D. Dr. Nolfi was the founder of the famous Danish health resort Humlegaarden and took pride in the fact that none of the guests at the spa ever had a cold.

Chop up a few cloves of garlic, wear them in a sac around your neck, and breathe in the vapors throughout the day.

Dian Dincin Buchman, noted investigator of natural medicine, was raised on home remedies. Whenever anyone in the family felt a cold coming on, it was time for *Molto Fino*, the name they called the salad that made that flu-ish feeling disappear. If someone was already sick, the salad helped the patient get better quickly.

As with lots of home remedies, there are no set measurements. Just know that you'll be divinely guided as you prepare the salad, and it will be perfect.

MOLTO FINO

Cut up tomatoes into small pieces, do the same with a chunk of onion—red, Vidalia, or yellow—add crushed garlic clove(s), some fresh-squeezed lemon juice, and a touch of virgin olive oil. Mix, eat, and feel better.

Irwin Ziment, M.D., professor of medicine at one of the country's most prestigious training grounds for physicians, the University of California School of Medicine, and chief of medicine and director of respiratory therapy at Olive View Medical Center in Los Angeles, is also an authority on pulmonary drugs. Who better to ask for the best cold/cough/chest congestion remedy? If you keep in mind Dr. Ziment's impressive credentials and imagine the research, experience, and expertise it took to earn those credentials, you will fully appreciate the value of the following remedy:

DR. ZIMENT'S GARLIC CHICKEN SOUP (a medicine)

Ingredients:

1 quart homemade chicken broth, *or* 2 cans low-fat, low-sodium chicken broth

1 garlic head, about 15 cloves, peeled

5 parsley sprigs, minced

6 cilantro sprigs, minced

1 teaspoon lemon pepper

1 teaspoon dried basil, crushed, *or* 1 tablespoon chopped
  fresh basil

1 teaspoon curry powder

Optional: hot red pepper flakes to taste, sliced carrots, a bay
  leaf or two

*Place all ingredients in a pot without a lid. Bring to a boil,
then simmer for about 30 minutes. If the soup is for your
own personal use, carefully inhale the fumes during preparation as an additional decongesting treatment. Remove
the solid garlic cloves and herbs and, along with a little
broth, puree them in a blender or food processor. Return
the puree to the broth and stir. Serve hot.*

Dosage: Take 2 tablespoons of Garlic Chicken Soup at the
beginning of a meal, one to three times a day. (If you feel you want
a little more than 2 tablespoons, fine, but do not exceed more than
1/2 cup at a time.)

CAUTION: Dr. Ziment cautions that this soup is a *medicine* and is
not to be eaten as one would eat a portion of soup.

Combine a crushed clove of garlic with 1/2 teaspoon of cayenne
pepper, the juice of 1 lemon, 1,000 mg of vitamin C (you can grind
the tablets or buy buffered vitamin C powder), and 1 teaspoon of
honey. Take this mixture three times a day at meals.

—If garlic is tough for you to take, even though you have a
cold and may not be able to taste anything, then peel and crush 6
cloves of garlic and mix them into 1/2 cup of white lard or petroleum jelly. Spread it on the soles of the feet. To keep the feet warm
and to prevent messing up your linens, put each foot in a plastic
bag, secure the bags by tying ribbon or cord around the ankles
(not too tight, you don't want to stop your circulation), and leave
it on overnight. It should help bring down a fever and clear up the
cold.

Garlic is so powerful that it will enter your system percuta-
neously (absorbed through the skin) and, even though it's applied
to one's feet, it will come out on one's breath. (Also see CONGES-
TION, NASAL CONGESTION, and Preparations chapter for
Soothing Garlic Syrups and Annemarie Colbin's Garlic/Miso Super
Soup for when you feel a cold coming on.)

COLD SORES . . . Rapid Relief

Speed up the healing process of a cold sore by cutting a clove of garlic in half and rubbing the juicy side on the sore. Or crush a clove and put it on the sore, keeping it in place with a bandage.

COLITIS . . . Remarkable Regularity Restorer

Colitis is a general term for inflammation of the large intestine. It can refer to a variety of irritable bowel problems resulting in extremes—diarrhea or constipation—and always a pain in the area. Since the symptoms can be quite severe, persistent, and debilitating, it is advisable to work with a professional health practitioner for proper diagnosis and as a consultant on a course of action. You may want to relay the following case histories to your doctor:

Rex Adams, medical reporter, cites the case of a man who suffered from chronic colitis. He began by taking 2 grams of garlic (1,000 mg = 1 gram) twice a day for 14 days, then reduced the dosage by half (2 grams of garlic once a day). Within the first few days he felt better. Three weeks later, he had two normal bowel movements daily.

Enterocolitis

This condition involves a swelling of both the small and large intestines. Rex Adams reports on a woman who was diagnosed as having acute enterocolitis. She took 2 grams of garlic three times a day, and by the fifth day her condition was perfectly normal.

CONGESTION . . . Nature's Roto Rooter

Congestion can build up in just about any part of the body—the digestive system, head, or chest. This can be the result of poor diet, addictive substances, improper medicinal drug use, and so on.

Lalitha Thomas's favorite approach for all varieties of congestion is a Garlic Enema (see Preparations chapter for instructions) combined with ingesting some form of garlic.

According to the experienced herbalist, "The garlic enema breaks up congestion throughout the body and helps the body to eliminate it. The use of garlic taken orally builds the immune system and helps restore equilibrium through its blood-purifying and antibiotic properties."

Lalitha cautions, "For chronic mucus congestion from an allergy or other regular irritation, remember that habitual use of enemas is not recommended." She suggests that you cleanse the blood and balance the diet to strengthen the functioning of the body as a whole.

Garlic, taken orally—as a cough syrup or garlic oil (see Preparations chapter)—also acts as an effective expectorant.

Lalitha reports superb results in clearing the severe congestion of ordinary pneumonia and "walking pneumonia" by using garlic orally, as an enema, and as a poultice (see Preparations Chapter) directly over the lungs. (Also see Dr. Ziment's Garlic Chicken Soup under COLDS/FLU and see NASAL CONGESTION.)

CONSTIPATION . . . The Stimulating Power of Allicin

Hippocrates, the Father of Medicine, recommended eating garlic (2 to 3 cloves) every day to help relieve constipation. The allicin in garlic is said to stimulate the peristaltic motion of the intestinal walls and in this way produces bowel movement.

Eat raw garlic in salads. Not only will the garlic help, but the fiber from the salad greens will go a long way in alleviating the condition. (See Recipes chapter for Garlic Herb Salad Dressing that will help lubricate your system.)

COUGHS . . .
Healing Homemade Soup, Syrup, Tea, and Lozenges

Take a teaspoon of garlic cough syrup (see Preparations chapter) when the cough acts up. Also sip garlic tea (see Preparations chapter) throughout the day. In addition to syrup and tea, eating raw garlic in soup and salad is also helpful in getting rid of mucus that may be causing the cough. (See Preparations chapter for Cough Syrups and Garlic Oxymel Lozenges.)

Bronchial Cough

In a glass, enamel, or porcelain pan, combine 4 cloves of minced garlic and an equal amount of petroleum jelly. Stir the mixture over low heat until the petroleum jelly is melted. Once the mixture cools, massage this garlicky paste into the chest and back to help clear up the congestion.

For a Cough That Accompanies a Cold, or Whooping Cough

Along with taking garlic internally in one or more forms (syrup, tea, capsules), this before-bedtime external remedy may prove very healing. Combine one part garlic juice with two parts soybean oil. Massage the mixture into the chest and back before you go to sleep. You may want to slip plastic wrap or cut-up plastic shopping bags under your sheet to protect the mattress from being oil-stained and smelling of garlic.

(*Also see* Dr. Ziment's Garlic Chicken Soup under COLDS/FLU, and see CONGESTION.)

CYSTITIS . . . The Magic of Nature's Own Infection Fighter

This terribly annoying condition is most often caused by a bacterial infection. In addition to taking at least 2 garlic capsules a day to help fight the infection, eat a couple of cloves of raw garlic and/or drink garlic tea (see Preparations chapter) throughout the day.

DEPRESSION . . . Garlic for a Natural High

During cholesterol and blood tests conducted on humans in Germany, scientific researchers became aware that the garlic-eating patients seemed to be in good spirits—less anxious and irritable. A theory is that garlic triggers the flow of serotonin, the chemical in the brain that can give one a sense of well-being. It may account for the fact that in Germany, the best-selling over-the-counter drugs are garlic supplements.

Introduce raw garlic into your diet, and start taking a supplement (follow the dosage on the label). Give it 2 weeks, then step
back and look at how you've been feeling. Don't focus on what's
been happening in your life, but on how you're coping with what's
happening in your life. Are you cheerier? Less moody? More hope-
ful? In general, do you have more of a sense of well-being rather
than a feeling of impending doom? Don't be surprised if you can
honestly answer yes. Garlic is known to be a mood elevator. (See
Garlic Express in Preparations chapter for a juiced garlic drink
that's an instant mood elevator.)

DIABETES . . . Blood-Sugar Level Reducer

Since garlic is known to reduce blood-sugar levels, it's a good idea
for diabetics to make sure garlic is part of their daily diet. The
addition of garlic should go along with professional health care,
constant monitoring, and, of course, a well-balanced, appropriate
diabetic diet.
    The combination of garlic, watercress, and parsley, eaten
daily, can help regulate the blood-sugar level. That's where *constant monitoring* is very necessary.

DIARRHEA and DYSENTERY . . .
Fast-Acting Stopper and Preventative

When you have an attack of diarrhea or dysentery, you will probably
be able to figure out or at least narrow down the cause of that attack.
Most bouts of diarrhea are due to poor digestion and eating food that
didn't agree with you, especially in a restaurant. You may have a mild
case of food poisoning. Nervous tension can also cause diarrhea.
    If you're traveling through exotic and primitive countries—
Southeast Asia, India, Mexico—and you've been drinking the
water or eating lettuce salads, you may have dysentery caused by
bacteria, protozoans, or parasites.
    When this problem strikes, you will not only know the cause,
you will also know the severity of the attack, where in the world

you are (the convenience of your home or the inconvenience of the New Zealand outback), and what you have access to. So, it will (as always) be up to you to determine your course of action, based on need and opportunity.

Before we present different suggestions on which to base your decisions, keep in mind that this should be a short-lived condition. If symptoms persist, be sure to see a health professional.

When you have a mild case of diarrhea or dysentery, a couple of garlic capsules taken twice a day, between meals, should do the trick. If it's more than mild, take 2 (500 mg) capsules three times a day, between meals. For a serious bout of the condition, take 2 (500 mg) capsules four times a day, between meals.

Add 1 finely chopped teaspoon of garlic to 1 teaspoon of honey and swallow it three times a day—2 hours after each meal. Or you may prefer to add the chopped garlic to a cup of clear broth. Some people opt for a cup of warm milk with the chopped garlic. Garlic in water is good, too. (Just be sure that it's not the water that gave you diarrhea.)

While visiting foreign lands, chances are your sightseeing will include outdoor markets. No doubt you will be able to stock up or replenish your supply of garlic. And that's a good thing so that at the first sign of amebic dysentery, you will be ready to start eating garlic—1 or 2 cloves—every few hours throughout the day. Herbalist Lalitha Thomas cautions you that after a bout of amebic dysentery, it is sometimes necessary to use raw garlic, in lesser doses, for up to a month to make sure the problem does not recur.

Prevention

Eating garlic daily is a good idea as a preventive measure. In this way, even if you do ingest some amebas or other parasites, they probably will not survive in your digestive tract.

Garlic, raw or in capsule form, in combination with acidophilus capsules (available at health food stores) is a favorite of many vacationing road warriors. While the garlic helps destroy viral and bacterial invaders, the acidophilus culture replaces and reinforces normal intestinal flora.

DIGESTION AND INDIGESTION . . .
Digestive-Enzyme Stimulator

Garlic has the wherewithal to discriminate between harmful and beneficial organisms, destroying the bad bacteria that may cause indigestion, without harming the good guys.

Garlic also helps stimulate the secretion of digestive enzymes, and it can relieve the problems that often accompany an upset stomach, such as heartburn and gas (unless you're one of the few who *get* heartburn and gas from garlic).

At the first sign of indigestion, take 2 garlic capsules or drink a cup of garlic tea (see Preparations chapter).

Garlic, as one of the ingredients *in* your food, may prevent indigestion before it starts. Or another preventive measure is 1/2 to 1 clove of finely minced raw garlic in 2 teaspoons of honey taken before meals.

DYSBIOSIS (Leaky Gut Syndrome) . . . Heartburn Helper

This condition exists when the lower esophageal sphincter doesn't close. According to complementary medicine specialist, Fred Pescatore, M.D:

> Several things may be used to treat the condition, like pancreatic enzymes, but garlic is the mainstay of treatment for leaky gut syndrome. The form to use is garlic oil (in the form of soft gels)—about 200 mg, three times a day, before each meal.

Compared to the dosage for high blood pressure, for example, the dosage for this health challenge is fairly low. Even so, each individual's history is important and has to be taken into consideration, since garlic can be an irritant and have the opposite effect, hurting the stomach. So, proceed with caution until you know your garlic tolerance level.

Dr. Pescatore puts his dysbiosis patients on a low carbohydrate/high protein diet. "Lowering the carbohydrate intake," says the

Doctor, "cuts down on the acidity in the stomach." The doctor is quick to add, "Many people can rid themselves of reflux (heartburn) just by cutting out the starches in their diet. A no-starch/no-sugar way of eating may make a tremendous difference in how you feel."

EARS . . .
Garlic: In One Ear and Out the Other

Earache

Garlic has antiviral and antibiotic properties that destroy many of the organisms that cause earaches.

When you have an earache, puncture a garlic pearle (soft gel) with a sterilized pin and squeeze the garlic oil into the painful ear. Gently plug the ear with a cotton ball.

There is a theory held by many health professionals that both ears should be treated even though only one ear has a problem. The reasoning is that it greatly reduces the chance of having the trouble transfer back and forth from ear to ear.

Natural healing therapist Alyce Finell shares this unique way of using garlic as a remedy for an earache: Thread a needle and stick it through the thick end of a peeled garlic clove. Unthread the needle, leaving the clove with both ends of the thread dangling. When you insert the clove—unthreaded end first—in the troubled ear, the thread will be hanging down the side of your neck. That thread is your assurance that the clove won't get lodged in the ear. Keep in overnight.

Alyce shared this remedy with a friend who had an inner ear infection and wasn't being helped by (expensive) prescription medication. The clove in the ear worked like magic.

You may want to coat the clove with vitamin E oil to protect the ear's delicate skin from a possible sensitivity reaction.

Ear Infection Prevention

Eat 1 to 2 cloves of garlic daily or take garlic supplements—follow the dosage on the label.

Children's Earache

For quick relief from the pain of an earache, moisten a small sterile cotton ball with warmed garlic oil (see Preparations chapter) and gently insert it in the child's ear.

To help prevent an ear infection from spreading throughout a child's system, use garlic as a natural antibiotic. Use a small peeled garlic clove that has been coated with vitamin E oil or castor oil, to protect sensitive skin from blistering or burning, and insert the clove in the child's rectum. Let it stay in overnight. The child will expel it naturally.

Wax Buildup

Warm a few drops of garlic oil (see Preparations chapter) and put it in the ear canal. Plug it with cotton and leave it there to soften the wax. After about an hour, flush the ear with water. Either stand under the shower, or use an infant enema syringe (available at most drugstores). Don't insert the syringe too far, you don't want to block the ear opening. It may take a lot of gentle flushing with warm water to break up and wash out the wax, so be patient.

Restore Partial Loss of Hearing

A loud noise, a cold, or wax buildup can cause partial loss of hearing. In Sicily, where garlic is considered a cure-all, they stew a few cloves in olive oil, then press it and strain it. On a daily basis, 3 or 4 drops of the warmed garlic/olive oil juice is placed in the ears and plugged up with cotton. It is said to help restore one's hearing.

This potent potion is *also* said to restore hearing: In a centrifugal juicer, juice garlic and onion so that you have 1 ounce of each. Combine the two and drink it once a day . . . *never* on an empty stomach. Since it's real strong stuff, you should fortify your innards with a meal or a serving of fat-free yogurt before drinking it.

Warning: Your juicer may never be the same. No matter how thoroughly you wash it, you can expect the next several juicings (that are not garlic and onion) to taste of garlic and onion.

Tinnitus (Ringing)

In a blender, combine 6 large peeled garlic cloves and 1 cup of almond oil or olive oil. Blend until the garlic is finely minced. Pour the mixture into a glass jar, put the cover on, and refrigerate it for 7 days. Then strain the liquid into an eyedropper bottle. Every evening, take the chill out of a small amount, then put 3 drops in each ear and plug the ears with cotton balls. Remove the cotton in the morning. Chances are, if it's going to stop the ringing, it will do so within 2 weeks. **Always keep this preparation refrigerated, and do not keep it longer than a month.**

EYE SPOTS (floaters) . . .
Helpful Vitamin-Absorbing Power of Garlic

The lack of B vitamins in one's system can cause problems with the optic nerves, resulting in *floaters*—annoying small particles *floating* around inside the eyes. Garlic helps increase the body's absorption of B vitamins tenfold. If you have floaters, you were probably told, "Nothing can be done about it. Learn to live with them."

A better suggestion is to learn to eat foods rich in B vitamins (brewer's yeast and whole grain cereals, for starters), to eat garlic, and to augment your daily food intake with B complex and garlic supplements.

FATIGUE . . .
A Wake-up Sniff and Drink

If you have a real bad case of the drowsies, puncture a garlic pearle (soft gel) and take a few deep whiffs, or cut a garlic clove in half and take some deep smells. That ought to wake you up.

Jimella Lucas and Nanci Main, participating at the annual Northwest Garlic Festival, share this energizing drink:

GARLIC PICK-ME-UP

Ingredients:

6 cloves garlic, peeled

3 tablespoons extra virgin olive oil

1/4 cup fresh lemon juice

6 ounces fresh orange juice

Optional: 3 ounces half & half (only if you need it to buffer the garlic, otherwise the additional fat and dairy are not recommended)

Place garlic in blender until chopped. Add the rest of the ingredients until blended. Pour into glass, and drink a little at a time. It's very potent!

Refrigerate any leftover drink.

The previous remedy is a temporary boost for the occasional late-afternoon can't-keep-your-eyes-open dip. If it's much more than just occasional fatigue, see your health professional.

FEET . . . Heal Heels, Toes, and a Corn That Grows

Treat yourself to Lalitha's Footbath (see Preparations chapter). According to the renowned herbalist Lalitha Thomas, the footbath will draw out toxins from the entire body, soothe tension and anxiety, rejuvenate sore or tired feet and legs, help treat athlete's foot (also see ATHLETE'S FOOT below), speed recovery from colds and flu (also see COLDS/FLU), relieve toxic buildup from a daily job environment that may be physically and/or emotionally polluted or stressful, and much, much more. And, it feels so good, too.

Athlete's Foot

This condition is a fungal infection that thrives in dark, warm, moist places like sweaty feet in socks and shoes.

The average pair of feet gives off a half-pint of perspiration daily, and it takes at least 24 hours for shoes to thoroughly dry after being worn. That's a good reason not to wear the same pair of shoes 2 days in a row, especially if you're prone to athlete's foot.

Avoid reinfecting your feet by wiping out your shoes with white vinegar. To be on the safe side, you might also rinse your socks with vinegar, as well as the bathtub, shower, and bathroom floor.

Apply 1 clove of crushed garlic to the affected area. Leave it on for a half-hour, then wash with water. If you do this once a day, within a week the condition may clear up completely.

CAUTION: When you first apply the garlic, there will be a sensation of warmth for a few minutes. If after a few minutes that warm feeling intensifies and the garlic is burning the skin, remove the garlic and wash the area with cool water. Next day, use garlic oil (see Preparations chapter) and try again.

Julian Whitaker, M.D., founder and president of the Whitaker Wellness Center in California, suggests that you put chopped garlic in your socks at bedtime and wear them overnight. Dr. Whitaker also recommends that people prone to athlete's foot should avoid eating yeast products, food that has vinegar as an ingredient, and all alcoholic beverages.

Garlic vinegar (see Preparations chapter) used externally may be successful in treating athlete's foot. With a cotton ball, swab the vinegar on the soles of your feet and between the toes. Air dry, then lightly brush cornstarch on your feet. Do this in the morning and at night.

Since garlic is a powerful fungus fighter, eating 1 or 2 cloves a day may help prevent athlete's foot or toenail fungus. (See TOE-NAIL FUNGUS. Also see Preparations chapter for FOOTBATH.)

Corns

Barbara Griggs, author of *The Green Witch Herbal*, suggests you circle the corn with a corn pad, then fill the hole above the corn with crushed garlic. Tape over and around it and keep it on overnight. Repeat the same procedure each evening until the corn softens and comes out.

FEVER . . . Bringing It Down With Sole Food

Please take into consideration that *fever* is a *symptom* of a health challenge—one that may need professional attention. With that in mind, garlic can be used—externally as well as internally—to help fight an infection that may be causing the fever.

Take garlic orally (see Nature's Amazing Antibiotic in the Preparations chapter) and/or peel and halve garlic cloves. Coat the bottom of your feet with a thin film of vitamin E or petroleum jelly, then either rub the cloves on the soles of the feet or bind them in place and keep them there overnight. Don't forget to put plastic or plastic wrap under your feet to protect the linens.

FINGERNAIL FUNGUS (See TOENAIL FUNGUS.)

FINGERNAILS . . .
Put an End to Thin, Breaking, and Splitting Nails

Raw garlic or garlic supplements taken daily along with vitamin B complex and zinc sulfate can help stop breaking, splitting, and thin fingernails. Zinc is also known to make white spots on fingernails disappear.

CAUTION: Prolonged use of zinc can cause copper deficiency.

GANGRENE . . . Emergency Measures to Save Life and/or Limb

The dictionary describes gangrene as the death and decay of body tissue, often occurring in a limb, caused by insufficient blood supply and usually following injury or disease.

As we mentioned in our introduction, neither one of us has a professional medical background. During our many years of experience with folk remedies—as writers, researchers, and reporters—this is the first time we're addressing this serious condition.

Given garlic's history, and how, during World War I, countless infected limbs of British military men were saved because medics knew to swaddle gangrenous wounds in garlic-soaked bandages, we would be remiss not to include limb-saving, if not life-saving garlic information to be used in an emergency situation, until you can get professional medical help.

So, as we've done throughout the remedy section of this book, we turn to the expertise of herbalist Lalitha Thomas, who advises:

> To prevent or possibly retard gangrene or blood poisoning, pack the entire area thickly with pulverized garlic directly in and around the wound. Clean out dead tissue and any pus, etc., with strong garlic water (see Preparations chapter). One way to do this is to soak the area for 10 minutes, and then repack it with a fresh garlic poultice (see Preparations chapter) at least three times a day. In some cases the red lines of blood poisoning actually begin retracting within a few hours, or at least by overnight. At this point in the process the dead gangrenous flesh may start cleaning out of the wound. With that the re-infection cycle is stopped, and the wound begins healing normally.

Considering the serious nature of this health challenge, we urge you to seek professional medical attention as soon as possible.

GARLIC BREATH . . . Fifteen Ways to De-Garlic Breath

Suck a lemon! Some people get better results when they add salt to the lemon, then suck it; some prefer to drink lemon juice after a little honey has been added. Or chew on a piece of orange peel. Or eat some lime sherbet.

The traditional herbal remedy for getting rid of garlic breath is "chewing parsley." Since parsley is often used as a garnish, it's usually readily available. If you don't like chewing parsley because of the way the little green pieces look in your teeth afterward, try sucking or chewing or swallowing any of the following breath sweeteners:

Fenugreek seeds

Coffee bean

Few roasted coffee grounds

Anise seeds

Mint leaf

Clove (the kind used to score a ham)

Cinnamon stick

Glass of milk

Or do as the French do, have some red wine.

PREVENTION: If you're taking raw garlic for medicinal pur-
poses and you don't want it on your breath, the secret is to finely
mince each clove and mix it into something so that you can swallow it without chewing it. After extensive experimentation, we've
found that finely minced garlic mixed into a dollop of fat-free
yogurt is best. Swallow it, a teaspooon of the mixture at a time.
The garlic doesn't stay on your breath, and the yogurt acts as a
buffer.

Finely minced garlic in apple sauce, honey, a glass of juice, or
in plain water, while not as soothing to your innards as yogurt, also
makes it easy to take, and will not give you garlic breath.

GOUT . . . Out! Out! Damned Gout With an Eating Regimen

Gout is a metabolic malady caused by the inadequate processing
of purines that break down, producing uric acid as a by-product.
The pain and swelling is caused when the uric acid converts to
sodium urate crystals that settle into joints and other tissues. To
help eliminate gout, add raw garlic to your diet . . . and eliminate
foods with purines.

Avoid: meat (especially organ meat), fish, shellfish (especially
clams, scallops, and mussels), fried foods, rich foods (desserts with
white flour, sugar, and cream), vegetables rich in purine (spinach,
peas, asparagus), consomme, broth, gravies, and mushrooms.

Have limited amounts only of: dried beans, lentils, cauliflower, poultry with as little fat as possible (no goose or duck or
poultry skin), oatmeal, yeast products.

Do have: Garlic! Eat two cloves of raw garlic daily. Since the
classic folk remedy for gout is cherries, mince the cloves and put
them in a glass of cherry juice. Be sure to get pure cherry juice or
concentrated juice that you dilute with water.

GUM PROBLEMS (gingivitis) . . .
A Remedy to Sink Your Teeth Into

Chances are, this conditon—red, swollen, and bleeding gums—is due to neglect, resulting in the buildup of bacterial plaque on the teeth. The time has come for professional periodontal help. Until you get to a periodontist, you may want to start taking garlic/parsley extract capsules (available at vitamin shops and health food stores). Take 2 every 4 hours for at least 3 days.

Raw garlic can clear up gum infections, but it can also *burn* your sensitive gums. Brian R. Clement, director of the Hippocrates Health Institute in West Palm Beach, Florida, reports that garlic is the first and foremost remedy for clearing up gum problems. Clement explains that the Institute's professional staff mixes pectin with garlic before impacting the gums with it. The garlic heals the infection while the pectin keeps it from burning the gums.

Suggest this line of defense to a (new age or holistic) periodontist.

HAIR . . . Garlic for Your Crowning Glory

Dandruff Prevention and Growth Stimulation

Herbalist Phillippa Back recommends this garlic lotion to improve the condition of one's hair.

Combine 1/2 cup vodka, 1/2 cup distilled water, and a medium-sized crushed garlic clove in a glass jar. Put the lid on and let it sit for 3 days. Then strain the liquid (lotion) into another glass jar and keep it covered. Once or twice a week, dampen a cotton ball with the lotion and gently rub it on the scalp.

Stopping Loss, Promoting Growth, Getting Rid of Gray

An hour before bedtime, slice open a clove of garlic and rub it on the area of the scalp where the hair is thinning. An hour later, massage the scalp with olive oil, put on a slumber cap, and leave it that way overnight. In the morning, shampoo. Repeat the procedure (night and morning) for at least 3 weeks. If, at the end of that time, it seems to you that this process has considerably slowed down or stopped hair from falling out and there is a regrowth in the previously sparse area, then continue with the program. If you don't seem to be making progress in that area, it's likely that the hair roots are not alive, and there's no use continuing this.

Medical research reporter Rex Adams offers a method of stimulating new hair growth and an explanation:

> Dice 2 cloves of garlic very finely, then mash the little pieces. Mix the garlic into a pint of 90 proof alcohol. Allow to stand for 2 days. Strain. Add 1 cup of fresh chopped burdock roots or flower heads. Allow to stand for 5 days. Strain. Sponge onto scalp every evening for a month. Reportedly, this is sufficient to promote hair growth.

Rex Adams's theory for the reason this works is twofold:

> First, as many doctors have acknowledged, garlic is a well-known rubefacient (capable of stimulating blood circulation, and also containing all the nutrients that hair follicles need), with strong penetrative powers. Second, the mineral content may have something to do with it. Garlic is rich in sulfur, and human hair contains lots of sulfur. Garlic also has zinc. When experimental animals are deprived of zinc in the diet, they invariably go bald.
>
> Garlic also contains copper. The graying of hair has been produced experimentally by a lack of copper. Finally, garlic increases your absorption of B vitamins when you eat foods that go well with it, and B vitamins have been found to cause hair to darken, in actual lab tests on scientists themselves.

HANGOVER . . . Symptom-Easing Gazpacho

Japanese scientists discoverd that feeding inebriated laboratory animals garlic sped up the process of clearing their bloodstream of alcohol and restored their loss of coordination.

Dosage for the maximum effect for the lab animals was equivalent to 5 to 15 cloves for the average-sized man. True, that amount of raw garlic may very well sober you up faster than usual or cut short the duration of the hangover, but if your garlic tolerance level is average, 5 to 15 cloves may irritate your stomach and compound your hangover headache. Instead—

Go with the suggestion of David E. Outerbridge, author of *The Hangover Handbook*: Gazpacho! Prepare this for the drinker the night before the morning after.

GAZPACHO

Ingredients:
1-1/2 pounds tomatoes
1 cucumber
2 scallions
1 green pepper
2 to 3 garlic cloves
3 tablespoons olive oil
1 small bunch parsley
salt, pepper, cayenne to taste

Chop all the vegetables into little pieces, add the olive oil and seasonings. Allow to stand for 12 hours. By that time, the drinker will be awake and ready for this remedy. Add cold tomato juice to bring the mixture to a proper consistency, and serve.

The garlic and the tomatoes are rich in potassium and vitamin C, which will help ease the symptoms of a hangover.

In ancient Rome, after Bacchanalian orgies, this hangover remedy saved the day . . . or the morning after:

HANGOVER REMEDY

Peel all the cloves of a head of garlic, add it to a pan with 10 ounces of red wine. Bring it to a boil, then simmer for 20 minutes. Strain, let it cool, then share it with your drinking buddy. No, it is not the hair of the dog. The alcohol evaporates, leaving tannic acid and garlic—a sobering combination.

HAY FEVER . . . Do-the-Trick Nosedrops

Garlic Water Nosedrops

Crush 1 clove of garlic into 1/4 cup hot water. When the water is
cool, strain the liquid into an eyedropper bottle. Put 10 drops of
this (mild) garlic water in each nostril three times a day for 3 days.
By the end of the third day—if not sooner—there should be a
noticeable clearing of the nasal passages, and you should be
breathing a lot easier.

If nose drops are not for you, take garlic and parsley pills—2
every 4 hours, four times a day for a few days, to help clear up your
hay fever or other pollen-related allergy that's affecting your sinus
area. (Also see ALLERGIES and SINUS.)

HEADACHE . . . Using Nature's Aspirin

This Early American headache remedy was said to be used by the
Pilgrims: Mix a teaspoon of honey with 1/2 teaspoon of garlic juice
and swallow it down at the start of a headache.

Alternating hot and cold garlic footbaths (see Preparations
chapter) have been known to make a headache—even a
migraine—disappear.

CAUTION: Too much garlic may *cause* a headache. It's rare, but it
has been known to happen.

A relative of ours felt that she was coming down with a cold.
To nip it in the bud, she roasted 3 bulbs of garlic, and in the course
of that day, ate all 3 bulbs.

That evening, she got a migraine headache. In examining her
lifestyle, diet, and the fact that she couldn't remember the last
time she had had a migraine, the only thing she could attribute it
to was the excessive amount of garlic she had consumed. When
she called and asked us if that was possible, we went to our files
and found several reports confirming the rare garlic-headache
connection.

Incidentally, the garlic our relative ate may have caused a
migraine, but it also circumvented the cold.

Headache With Pinging

Chances are you will not find this term in a medical dictionary. But if you're one of those who gets a *pinging* sensation as part of a headache, you'll be happy to know that garlic has been known to put an end to those *stabbing* or *shooting* pains. And why not? According to medical research reporter Rex Adams:

> Garlic is nature's aspirin, dilating the veins and arteries—letting blood through—and could dissolve fatty deposits on artery walls, preventing clogging. Garlic also increases the body's absorption of vitamin B-1 (thiamin) tenfold, the vitamin that's vital to nerve health, and the lack of which may be somewhat responsible for the pings. So, along with garlic, take a daily B-1 supplement.

HEART . . . Garlic: The Smart-Heart Herb

According to noted medical researcher and reporter Carlson Wade:

> Garlic eases plaque formation in arteries; it is a prime source of allicin, an active sulfur-containing compound that is changed into diallyl-disulfide in the system; this helps to liquefy cholesterol deposits, loosen plaque, reduce lipid (fat) levels in the blood and liver, and improve the action of the heart. Garlic also improves the flow of oxygen into the bloodstream, thereby relieving chest pain associated with heart conditions. (Medically, the condition is call angina pectoris, in which the heart muscle receives an insufficient blood supply, causing pain in the chest and often in the left arm and shoulder.) It is garlic that may well help to dilate the blood vessels, allow a better exchange of oxygen, and relieve pain.

So, have a heart . . . a healthy heart . . . take garlic!

Ray C. Wunderlich, Jr., M.D., of the Wunderlich Center for Nutritional Medicine in St. Petersburg, Florida, says that he gives his patients hawthorn, which he believes to be the number-one agent for the cardio-vascular system, along with garlic. Garlic acts as a catalyst for the hawthorn's effectiveness:

> The two are a good combination. They sort of work in tandem. It doesn't happen immediately. Over time—weeks, maybe months—hawthorn can completely restructure and improve the heart and the blood vessel function. A good dose must be taken consistently. Most people don't have any trouble taking hawthorn capsules—500 mg, 2 at a time, twice a day (that's a total of 4 a day, totaling a daily intake of 2 grams). The same dosage of garlic should be taken (4 [500 mg] capsules) along with the hawthorn each day.

(*Also see heart-related conditions:* BLOOD PRESSURE, CHOLESTEROL, ARTERIOSCLEROSIS AND ATHEROSCLEROSIS, and STROKE PREVENTION.)

HEMORRHOIDS . . . A Clove a Day Where the Sun Don't Shine

In the morning, apply garlic oil (see Preparations chapter) *externally*.

For *internal* use, peel a clove of garlic (be careful not to bruise it) and, ideally, right after a bowel movement, insert it in the rectum as you would a suppository. Leave it in overnight or until your next elimination. Garlic will help disinfect the area and bring down the swelling. Repeat the procedure daily until you're hemorrhoid-free.

HEPATITIS . . . Prevention and Treatment Until You Get Help

The type of hepatitis referred to here is the inflammation of the liver caused by ingesting contaminated food or water. It is a good idea to eat garlic daily, especially while traveling, to help prevent this liver disease. (Check GENERAL DOSAGE for daily amount when traveling in high-risk areas.)

This serious condition should be treated immediately by a health professional. However, if you do contract hepatitis, especially if you are in an out-of-the-way place with no reliable medical treatment, it is advisable to take garlic every hour or two, depending upon the seriousness of the case. **CAUTION: Get reliable medical help as soon as possible!**

HERPES (genital and oral) . . . Nature's Preventative

Thanks to its antiviral properties, a daily dose of garlic is said to prevent outbreaks of genital or oral herpes.

On active sores, a garlic bath may help, or you may find healing relief by applying a mild poultice on the area. (See Preparations chapter for Bath and Poultice instructions.)

IMMUNE SYSTEM . . . A Three-Ingredient Power Potion

The immune system defends the body against external invasions, and it also seeks out and destroys defective or mutinous cells in the body, such as cancer cells. Many biological sulfhydryl compounds and polysulfides can stimulate immune function. Garlic is rich in these compounds. And so it should come as no surprise that research scientists are finding that garlic boosts the body's immune system.

Tarig Abdullah, M.D., and his team of investigators at the Akbar Clinic and Research Center in Panama City, Florida, are involved in garlic research. One promising area of their research has to do with strengthening the immune defenses in AIDS patients.

Meanwhile, it is reported that Dr. Abdullah eats a couple of cloves of raw garlic daily, and since he started doing that, has not had a cold. Did we mention when the doctor started his daily garlic-eating ritual? It was in 1973.

We start our day by drinking a full glass of water, followed by a teaspoon of cod liver oil and a whole clove

*of garlic. A whole, raw clove—that's right. Garlic is
good for preventing colds, and it's good for your bowels. We chop the clove as finely as we can, then scoop
it up with a spoon, and swallow it all at once, without chewing, to prevent odor. We wash it down with
one glass of cold water, then one glass of hot water.*

—Sarah L. Delany (age 104) and
—A. Elizabeth Delany (age 102)
Having Our Say: The Delany Sisters' First 100 Years

Much has been written about the healing properties of honey
as well as apple cider vinegar. And we already know about garlic.
Here's a recipe combining all three ingredients:

IMMUNE-BOOSTING POWER-PACKED POTION

*In a blender's container, pour 1 cup apple cider vinegar, 1
cup honey (raw is best), and 8 cloves peeled, chopped garlic. Mix on high for 1 minute. Pour the mixture into a glass
jar, cover tightly, and refrigerate. After 5 days, the potion is
ready. The recommended dosage is 2 teaspoons daily after
breakfast. (Always keep it refrigerated.)*

IMPETIGO . . . Fast Healing Relief

This contagious bacterial skin infection usually starts on the face
as a redness and progresses to itching blisters that turn into crusty
lesions. Get out the garlic! Take it internally for its power as an
antibiotic, and put it on the affected area in the form of garlic oil
(see Preparations chapter).

IMPOTENCE . . . A Simple Test and a Stimulating Treatment

Is the problem physical or psychological? To help you determine
the answer to that question, there's a simple test you can take.
(How appropriate that the word *test* is part of this, since it's from
the Latin root that means "to witness," and it's the same Latin root

from which the word *testes*—the pair of male gonads that produce semen—is derived.) Enough irony—let's get to the test.

The test is based on the fact that most men have about five erections every night in their sleep. No matter how uptight they may be, and no matter what trouble they may be having with erections while awake, men who suffer from *psychological* impotency will have firm erections every night in their sleep.

To test for these erections, get a roll of postage stamps (you can buy the least expensive stamps as long as they come in a roll). At bedtime, wrap the stamps in a single thickness around the shaft of the penis. Tear off the excess stamps, then tape the two ends (the first and the last stamps) around the penis, firmly but not too tight. Pleasant dreams . . . really.

When a nighttime erection occurs, the increased diameter of the penis should break the stamps along the line of one of the perforations. If there is a physical (organic) reason for impotency, you will not have nightly erections and the stamps will be intact in the morning.

This "stamp act" should be repeated every night for a couple of weeks. If the stamps are intact every morning, there most likely is a *physical* problem, and you should see a specialist for scientific tests and proper diagnosis.

> *Garlic may be, as some folklore would have it, an aphrodisiac, but does it seem likely that a turn-on could be at one and the same time such a turn-off?*
>
> —Malcolm Forbes, Sr.

If, each morning, the stamps are broken along a perforation, chances are you have a normal capability for having erections and impotency is *psychologically* caused. Sometimes just knowing that everything is working well organically will give you the confidence and assurance you need to help you rise to the occasion. To give you that extra *oomph*, you may want to try garlic.

Garlic is said to stimulate sexual desire and the production of semen. In fact, in some religious orders of monks and nuns, garlic is eliminated from their diet for that reason.

If you're not in one of those orders, you may want to eat raw garlic in salads and use it in cooking and/or take 2 garlic pills daily.

Hey, knowing what a big part garlic plays in Italian and French cuisine, and considering the reputation of Frenchmen and Italians, there seems to be something to it.

A Lithuanian folk remedy combining garlic with the fermented juice of grapes is said to produce a powerful potion that may stir feelings that were dormant for a long time. Add peeled, crushed garlic cloves to a bottle of wine—1 teaspoon of garlic for each cup of wine, then refrigerate the bottle. Take 1 teaspoon of the wine five times a day.

CAUTION: This is an alcoholic beverage. If you are on medication or have any kind of alcohol intolerance, this is clearly *not* for you.

Respected French folk herbalist Maurice Messegue advised his on-in-years patients who were having problems to massage the coccyx (tailbone) at the base of the spinal column for about 10 minutes a day, in a circular motion, with crushed cloves of garlic. It is reported that about 40 percent of Monsieur Messeque's patients were no longer troubled by impotence after using this remedy.

INFECTIONS . . . Garlic, the Supreme Combatant

Dr. Fred Pescatore, complementary medicine specialist, has used garlic on patients who have peripheral edema and have gotten superficial cellulitis (infections of the skin that usually stay in one place) oozing from their legs, and who refuse to be on antibiotics. The doctor says that a lot of his patients refuse to be on antibiotics. For those individuals, Dr. Pescatore advises them to grind up garlic, mix it with castor oil, and make a poultice (see Preparations chapter)—then place it on the sores to help heal them.

For a minor rash or infection, the treatment of choice would be a dusting of garlic powder (bought in bulk at an herb store). For more serious infections, check it out with your health professional. Until you do, you can place a heavier application of garlic powder on the area and cover with a cotton bandage, or use a garlic poultice (see Preparations chapter).

For a small patch of skin infection rub the juicy half of a garlic clove on it several times a day.

Dian Dincin Buchman, Ph.D., author, and renowned investigator of natural medicines, has given us her Anti-Infection Wash (see Preparations chapter). It can be taken internally to help fight infection. The dosage is a teaspoon in between meals, one to three times a day. (Also see WOUNDS and YEAST INFECTION.)

INSECT BITES . . . Stop the Itching; Start the Healing

Cut a peeled clove of garlic in half and rub it over the insect bite several times. If it's a real troublesome bite, crush the half clove of garlic and leave it on the bite, securing it in place with a bandage or handkerchief.

In parts of the Middle East, a peeled clove of garlic is chewed and mixed with one's own saliva, then applied directly on the bite or sting.

Thyme Garlic Vinegar

You might want to have this Gypsy solution on hand to relieve the itch and help eliminate the heat, redness, and swelling. It takes a moon (a month) to prepare, so put it up in the spring and you'll be ready when mosquito season arrives.

In a clean, clear, screwtop jar, pour in 1 pint of apple cider vinegar, and add 3 tablespoons of fresh thyme or 1 tablespoon of the dried herb. Close the jar as tightly as possible and place it in a warm spot (on a window ledge in the sun). Each morning and each evening, shake the jar vigorously. After a half-moon (2 weeks) add 7 crushed garlic cloves to the mixture. Let it steep for another half-moon in the same place, and continue shaking it each morning and evening. At the end of the month, strain the liquid into a *dark* bottle and keep it in a dark, cool place. At the first sign of an insect bite, apply this Thyme Garlic Vinegar to the area.

INSECT REPELLENT . . . The Great Shoo-er

Biologist Eldon L. Reeves of the University of California tested garlic extract on five species of mosquitoes. Not one mosquito survived.

Mosquitoes and just about all other insects despise garlic. If you're going into a bug-infested area, wear garlic around your neck, on top of your clothes. Simply take strong thread and a needle, and string a strand of cloves. Make it long enough to put on over your head. Or, you may prefer to turn the strand of cloves into a hat band. Incidentally, there's no need to peel the cloves. That way you won't smell the garlic, but the insects will, and they'll stay away.

Camping out? Take garlic powder with you. At night, if it's not windy, sprinkle the powder around your sleeping bag. Under windy conditions, fill little net bags with garlic cloves and tie them to the corners of your sleeping bag.

Ants

If you have an ant problem in your home, or on a windowsill, or out on the patio, rub a peeled clove of garlic along their trail and the area will be ant-free in no time.

INSOMNIA . . . A Relaxing Lead-In to a Good Night's Z-Z-Z-Z-Z

According to research reports, too much garlic may actually cause insomnia. How much is "too much"? Only you can determine that for yourself. For a few days, cut out or cut down on your daily garlic intake and see if that makes a difference in terms of a good night's sleep. If you no longer have insomnia, it hurts us to say this but, you may have been eating too much garlic. Gradually add garlic back into your diet and, during the process, pay attention to your sleep patterns. That way, you'll be able to regulate the amount of garlic your system can take before it starts affecting your sleep.

If, after testing your garlic consumption in relation to your insomnia, you are convinced that garlic has nothing to do with it, then take a garlic bath (see Preparations chapter) right before going to bed. It just may put an end to sleepless nights of tossing and turning.

An alternative to taking a garlic bath is to coat the soles of the feet with a thin layer of castor oil or petroleum jelly, then rub the same areas with the juicy side of a peeled half-clove of garlic. Do the same thing—coating and rubbing—on the nape of your neck. Many insomniacs—*former* insomniacs—say this worked after all else failed.

JOCK ITCH . . . Destroying the Fungus Among Us

This is a fungal infection of the groin, and it's contagious. Don't scratch it—you can spread it to other parts of your body, including your scalp (see RINGWORM).

Puncture a garlic pearle (soft gel) and squish the oil on the itchy patch. If possible, do it three times a day until it clears up completely.

To eliminate the ideal conditions for growing fungus, wear loose-fitting cotton underwear to keep air in and moisture out.

If you don't have a problem with raw garlic, Dr. Julian Whitaker, founder and president of the Whitaker Wellness Center in California, advises eating as much raw garlic as possible at the first sign of jock itch. If you just can't tolerate raw garlic, take a garlic capsule after every meal.

Dr. Whitaker also thinks it's a good idea to avoid yeast products such as breads, baked goods, and alcohol. They may make some people more prone to getting jock itch.

LEAD POISONING AND OTHER HEAVY METALS . . . Important Detox Program for the Entire Family

Teething on painted furniture is not the only way lead and other toxic heavy metals get into our system. Does your home have *copper* piping? Are you cooking in aluminium pots? Did your dentist fill your cavities with mercury? Even if you answered no to those questions, if you live in America, chances are you inhale fumes from cars that use leaded gasoline. That's the bad news. The good news is: studies show that garlic helps prevent and treat poisoning from heavy metals. It is for that very reason in lead factories in China, the factory workers eat 2 raw cloves of garlic twice a day.

Eat garlic often! If you have children, give them garlic, too. It goes great on pizza, either in powder form or roasted, or raw, finely minced. Garlic supplements also help. (Also see POLLUTION.)

LEAKY GUT SYNDROME (See DYSBIOSIS.)

LIVER DISEASE PREVENTION . . .
Drinking a Daily Liver Flush

To help cleanse the liver, and promote a healthier elimination system, California herbalist Jennifer Moore recommends drinking this Liver Flush daily, one-half hour before breakfast:

LIVER FLUSH

Combine the juice of 2 oranges and 1 lemon, 2 or 3 chopped or pressed garlic cloves, and 2 tablespoons cold-pressed olive oil. Mix vigorously, and drink.

The bonuses of a healthy liver are good skin tone, better hair texture, and lots more energy.

LYME DISEASE . . . Possible Prevention That's Worth a Try

Possible Prevention

Under INSECT REPELLENTS we suggest a garlic clove necklace or hatband. To repel Lyme ticks, how about garlic clove ankle bracelets tied around the bottom of pant legs? It may serve as double protection: to prevent the little buggers from crawling up your leg and to repel them completely.

To Speed Recovery

Founder of the Whitaker Wellness Center in California, Julian Whitaker, M.D., says, "Garlic is a generalized antibiotic, which may help you get over Lyme disease more quickly." Dr. Whitaker also recommends foods rich in vitamin C—citrus fruits, cantaloupe, kiwis, papaya, berries, green peppers, and most green leafy vegetables—for quick relief from the Lyme disease's flulike symptoms.

MASTITIS . . . Enhanced Garlic Formula

Mastitis is an inflammation of lymph and/or mammary glands in the breast. The two common kinds are: acute mastitis, involving bacterial infection, and chronic mastitis, with no infection, just tenderness and pain.

If you think this is your problem, we urge you to check with a trusted health professional for proper diagnosis and treatment. Treatment usually consists of antibiotics. You may want to take this book with you to your doctor and show her or him the information on garlic as an antibiotic. While you're waiting for your doctor's appointment, take the Enhanced Garlic Formula (see Preparations chapter under Nature's Amazing Antibiotic).

MELANOMA . . . Can't Argue With Success

We said it before, we'll say it again: We're writers who do research. We have no professional medical background. We're reporting and not prescribing. We urge you to seek out, find, and work with a health professional whose approach to your well-being is in keeping with your own. You want a doctor who is not in the panic business—someone who can properly diagnose the health challenge, then discuss the conventional, complementary, and alternative options for whatever ails you.

If you see a beauty mark on your body that has an irregular border and whose color seems to move beyond that border, or there's a nodelike dark patch of skin that's changing in size, we think it's very important that you show it to your doctor.

And now that we're on record with our suggestion, we're *reporting* the experience of Bill Anderson, managing partner of Garlic Research Labs and Garlic Valley Farms, with what he thought may have been melanomas.

In the course of doing business, Bill Anderson comes into contact with lots of farmers. Here are Bill's own words:

> One day, one of those farmers told me about a melanoma that he had on his lip. The farmer took a garlic clove, sliced it, and put it on the melanoma, then covered it with a bandage. From time to time, he'd change the gar-

lic clove and put on a new bandage. Within two weeks the thing on his lip completely disappeared. Another time this farmer had a melanoma on the back of his neck. He did the same thing and sure enough, it also disappeared completely.

While Bill was leading up to his own experience, he shared this one, too:

I had dealings with this ol' country lady in Little River, who worked in a feed store. She told me, "Oh yeah, that garlic is good for everything. Here we use it for skin cancer. We had this one farmer who had it on his arm. He drives a tractor and the arm is always out in the sun. The doctor said he couldn't do nothin' for him, so I mixed up some onions and garlic and made a mince out of it and rubbed it all over his arm, then I wrapped it up. In two weeks the skin cancer was all gone."

The time had come for Bill's own personal story:

I had this black mole on my neck for a couple of years. It kept getting bigger. When it was about the size of a penny, only fatter—that thing was real ugly—I got to thinkin' about the success the farmers had getting rid of their problem, and said, "Hell, I'll put some of my own garlic juice on there." [Bill's company, Garlic Valley Farms, bottles and sells 99.3 percent pure garlic juice.] I dipped my finger down into the bottle and smeared it on, just that one time. In a little over a week, maybe close to two weeks, the thing on my neck disappeared. Then I got the same thing on my right temple. I put the garlic juice on it and it also disappeared. It's the God's truth.

In the 1850s, Louis Pasteur recognized garlic's ability to kill bacteria. More than a century later, biochemist Sidney Belman of New York University Medical Center reported that by painting garlic oil on the skin of laboratory animals, he could inhibit the development of skin cancers. Extensive research continues, with extremely encouraging results.

MEMORY . . . A First Lady's Extraordinary-Memory Secret

Eleanor Roosevelt was known to have an exceptionally good memory. When she was quite on in years, she was asked to what she attributed her great memory. Her answer was, "three cloves of garlic a day." Rumor has it that Mrs. Roosevelt dipped the garlic cloves in either honey or chocolate.

In *Stop Aging Now!*, health and nutrition authority, Jean Carper says, "Japanese experiments on animals indicate that garlic constituents protect neurons from damage and act as growth factors to stimulate the branching of brain cells. Giving aged garlic extract (Kyolic) to old animals restored some mental functions, including memory and problem-solving abilities."

Jean Carper also reports on the encouragingly optimistic work of Dr. Hiroshi Saito, professor of pharmaceutical sciences at the University of Tokyo, who has screened dozens of natural and synthetic products in a search for new drug treatments for senile dementia, whose findings lead him to believe that garlic may even help prevent and reverse Alzheimer's-like senility.

MENOPAUSE . . . Symptom-Easing Relief

A warm half garlic bath (see Preparations chapter), 10 minutes once or twice a day, can be beneficial and soothing to a woman who is troubled by the bothersome symptoms of menopause.

Eat a couple of cloves of garlic, and take a vitamin B-complex daily. Garlic increases the absorption of B vitamins, and they're helpful in relieving hot flashes, chills, irritability, and other unpleasant symptoms of menopause.

MENSTRUATION . . . Monthly Management

PMS

Eat 1 or 2 cloves of garlic, or take garlic supplements along with a B-complex vitamin daily. Garlic helps the absorption of B vitamins and therefore can help eliminate PMS symptoms such as anxiety, nausea, headache, tiredness, mild depression, abdominal bloating, and breast tenderness.

Menstrual Cramps

For the first couple of days when period pains are at their worst, take 4 or 5 garlic capsules throughout the day and night—1 after each meal, 1 between lunch and dinner, and 1 before going to bed. The rest of the month, take 2 or 3 garlic capsules daily.

To Regulate a Weak Flow

Take alternating hot/cold garlic footbaths (see Preparations chapter).

Also, since garlic is a proven emmenagogue (it stimulates the menstrual flow) add 1 or 2 garlic cloves to your daily diet.

MORNING SICKNESS (See PREGNANCY.)

MUSCLE SORENESS AND STIFFNESS (Charley Horse) . . . Wash Away Pain

(See Preparations chapter for Dian Dincin Buchman's formula for Anti-Infection Wash and Arthritis Pain Liniment.)

MUSCLE SPASMS . . . Easing the Tension

Garlic is known to be a powerful antispasmodic. If you have tension that's causing muscle spasms, take garlic in some form: raw, capsules, pearles (soft gels), or powder. Along with the addition of garlic to your daily diet, take calcium lactate or calcium gluconate—follow the dosage on the label.

NAIL FUNGUS (See TOENAIL FUNGUS.)

NASAL CONGESTION . . . Clearing the Passages With Fumes

Combine 3 cloves of chopped garlic and 2 teaspoons of vinegar in a pot with 1 pint of just-boiled water. Put a lid on the pot and let the garlic steep for about 5 minutes. Then remove the lid and carefully inhale the fumes. It should help clear your nasal passages and give you temporary relief. (Also see ALLERGIES, CONGESTION, HAY FEVER, and SINUS.)

NECK . . . Getting Rid of the Pain in the Neck

Neck Gravel

When you roll your neck around or just turn from side to side, if you hear and feel that there's gravel in there, it's time to do some neck rolls. Start with your chin on your chest and slowly rotate your head so that your right ear reaches for your right shoulder, then head back, left ear to left shoulder, and back with your chin on your chest. Do these rolls, slowly, six times in one direction and six times in the opposite direction, morning and evening. Also eat 3 to 4 cloves of raw garlic a day or take a garlic capsule after each meal. As the tension in your neck is released, and as the garlic builds up in your system, the gravelly noise in your neck should gradually disappear.

Stiff Neck

Educator-author Andrew H.Y. Kim suggests you make a poultice using 3 large peeled and minced cloves of garlic mixed with 1 cup of flour and rolled into a piece of light-weight white cotton fabric. (A handkerchief would be good.) Place the poultice on the lower part of the neck, almost resting on the uppermost part of the shoulders, and let it stay there until the mixture dries completely. You can expect a tingly feeling at first, but that should ease up, just as your stiff neck should.

NERVOUS TENSION/STRESS . . . Chill Out, Naturally

Many herbalists suggest garlic as an effective nervine because it's known to help a person calm down and de-stress at the same time. The advised dosage for prevention or treatment is at least 2 raw cloves a day. If raw garlic is not a viable option, take at least 2 (500 mg) garlic supplements a day. This garlic treatment should be combined with a balanced diet devoid of refined sugars and processed foods. (If your nervous tension shows up as muscle spasms, see MUSCLE SPASMS.)

NIGHTMARES (children's) . . .
An Intriguing Remedy That Works Like a Dream

Herbalist-author David Carroll suggests that when a child wakes in the night from nightmares, give the child a whiff of perfume or cologne to dispel the memory of the nightmare. Then rub garlic on the soles of the feet to prevent more bad dreams. We suggest that you first coat the child's soles with a thin layer of petroleum jelly. Also, to protect the bedding somewhat, put socks on the child's feet.

NOSEBLEED . . . Garlic—And Step on It!

CAUTION: If blood is flowing from both nostrils, it may not be a simple nosebleed. Get professional medical attention immediately.
     For the average one-nostril nosebleed, first, gently blow your nose to clear out all the blood you can, making it easier to clot. Then, peel and mince about 3 garlic cloves and put them in the middle of a 6-inch square of cheesecloth. Gather the corners and put a plastic tie around it, creating a little bag of garlic. Put a piece of plastic on the floor and put the cheesecloth-wrapped garlic on it, smooth side up. If your *right* nostril is bleeding, place the instep of your *left* foot on the garlic. If your *left* nostril is bleeding, place the instep of your *right* foot on the garlic. Leave it there until your nose stops bleeding. If it doesn't stop bleeding within 10 minutes, take other steps.

PNEUMONIA . . . What to Do Until the Doctor Comes

Pneumonia is a condition caused by viruses and bacteria moving into the lungs causing infection, inflammation, and congestion. **CAUTION: Seek professional medical attention immediately!**

While help is on the way, a garlic poultice (see Preparations chapter) placed on the patient's chest can be very healing. Or, peel and crush a bulb of garlic. Put the cloves in a pan, cover with water (distilled, spring, or at least filtered water) and bring to a boil. Turn off the heat and let it steep until it's cool enough to touch. Soak a white washcloth in the warm garlic water, wring it out and place it directly on the patient's chest. When the cloth is no longer warm, reheat it by redipping it in the garlic water. Wring it out and place it on the patient's chest again. Keep repeating the process until the doctor comes. Also, finely mince a clove of garlic, put it in water or juice and urge the patient to drink it.

POISON IVY . . . Stop the Itching; Start the Healing

If you realize that you just brushed up against poison ivy and you can get to cold water within 3 minutes, you can wash away the nasty oil. *Do not use soap.* One theory is that the oil from the soap can seal in the poison ivy oil, and the other theory is that the soap will remove the acid mantle that protects the skin.

If you're unaware of getting poison ivy until you're home and it starts to itch, chop 4 peeled cloves of garlic and boil them in 1 cup of water. After the mixture cools, dip a white washcloth in it, wring it out a little, then apply it to the poison ivy areas. Each time the cloth dries, repeat the process.

Prevention

Go to the library and find a book that has pictures of poison ivy. Take note of the thin, pale stems with three leaves on each stem. Next time you see what you think is poison ivy, try the white paper test. Using a piece of white paper, take hold of the plant-in-question and crush the leaves. If it's poison ivy, in about 5 minutes, the juice on the paper will turn black.

Getting Rid of the Plant

Never get rid of a patch of poison ivy by burning it. The plant's oil gets in the air. Inhaling it can be harmful. Instead, while wearing gloves, uproot the plants and leave them on the ground to dry out in the sun. Or, prepare a solution of 3 pounds of salt in a gallon of soapy water. Spray the poison ivy plants over and over.

Note: Tools that are used for digging up poison ivy plants should be thoroughly washed with the (above) solution. When you're finished destroying the poison ivy and cleaning your tools, carefully take off your gloves, turning them inside out, and dispose of them. You may need to toss your clothes away also, since the poison ivy oil may not wash out completely and can stay active for at least a year.

POLLUTION . . .
What You Should Know If You Breathe Outdoors

Dian Dincin Buchman, renowned investigator of natural medicine, shares her pollution solution:

> In addition to my personal dose of minerals and vita- mins, I take large amounts of vitamin C, vitamin E, cal- cium citrate, and organic garlic capsules. All these sub- stances help to overcome the effects of smog, nitrogen dioxide, and ozone toxicity.

Dr. Buchman reports that Dr. Michael Walczak, Editor-in- Chief of the Journal of Applied Nutrition, comments on the value of disulfide compounds in protecting us against ozone pollution and avoiding any possible nitrogen dioxide and smog pollution. This compound is readily available to the body through the use of organic garlic extract, because garlic is high in sulfur. (Also see LEAD POISONING.)

PREGNANCY . . . More Stamina, Easier Delivery—
and a Second Opinion

According to British childbirth writer Sheila Kitzinger, if you eat garlic and onions on a regular basis, starting in your third month of pregnancy, your stamina will increase and delivery will be easier. Here's the scientific explanation that you may want to discuss with your doctor: The linoleic acids in both garlic and onion help produce prostaglandins that help stimulate cervical effacement and dilation.

A Second Opinion

Naturopathic Doctor Mildred Jackson says,

> Pregnant women and nursing mothers should *not* eat the following foods as they can cause gas and colic in the mother and, consequently, the baby: garlic, cauliflower, cabbage, onions, broccoli, and excess quantities of beans.

Morning Sickness

Garlic enhances the absorption of vitamin B-1 (thiamine), the vitamin that has been known to help relieve morning sickness. Check with your obstetrician for permission to take vitamin B-1 and garlic, and for the recommended dosage.

PREMENSTRUAL SYNDROME (PMS) (See MENSTRUATION.)

PROSTATE . . . Infection Protection

Years ago, noted health and nutrition writer Carlson Wade explained how garlic keeps the prostate free of infection:

> Volatile garlic is a powerhouse of natural antibiotics that help to insulate your prostate against the risk of infectious bacteria. A European electrobiologist, Professor Gurwitch, discovered that garlic releases a form of ultraviolet radiation called mitogenetic radiations. These emissions, now referred to as *Gurwitch rays* in the scientific world, have the ability of stimulating cell growth and activity of the prostate gland. Garlic would then appear to have this natural antibiotic property that

would (1) shield the prostate against parasitic infections and (2) repair and reconstruct weakened glandular tissues so they give one a healthy organ.

Garlic is a prime source of allicin, a substance believed to help cleanse away decomposed bacteria that might otherwise cause prostatic infection.

As of this writing, a paper by research scientists is in the process of being published in a medical journal about the impressive benefits of garlic on laboratory animals with prostate cancer. Extensive tests by the same researchers have already begun on human cells.

PSORIASIS . . . Juice Your Way to Relief

A Chinese folk remedy recommends that you dab garlic juice on the patches of psoriasis. Good results have also been reported by puncturing garlic pearles (soft gels) and squeezing out the oil on the affected areas. Apply either the garlic juice or garlic oil at least once a day; twice—morning and evening—would be best.

RINGWORM . . . A Potent Cleanser

Finely mince 2 peeled cloves of garlic and mix them together with the oil from 3 punctured vitamin E pearles (soft gels). Spread the mixture on the infected area three times a day to stop the itching and start the healing.

SCIATICA . . . Five Ways to Be Pain-Free

Sciatica is a swelling of or injury to the sciatic nerve, causing pain, soreness, and/or tingling. Since the sciatic nerve starts at the base of the spine and travels down the thigh and leg to the foot, the pain can be as extensive as the nerve.

1. Sciatic pain may be caused by a misalignment in the body. If that's the case, professional help would then be needed to

adjust the alignment. If that's *not* the case, bed rest and heat in the form of hot baths (see Preparations chapter) and heating pads are usually recommended for sciatica. Here are a couple of other recommendations:

2. Each morning and evening, mince 2 peeled cloves of garlic, put them in 1/2 cup milk and drink it down. It has been reported that after a few days of this garlic/milk regimen, you should feel some relief. Within 2 weeks, all the pain should be gone.

3. According to the *Pakistan Medical Times*, vitamin B-1 and garlic are very beneficial. Eat garlic raw in salads and use it in cooking. Also, take 2 garlic capsules a day, plus 10 mg of vitamin B-1 along with a potent vitamin B complex. Garlic greatly enhances the absorption of the B vitamins.

4. For a *hot* liniment with which to rub the painful area, use Dian Dincin Buchman's formula for her Anti-Infection Wash and Arthritis Pain Liniment (see Preparations chapter).

5. Ancient Roman doctors treated sciatica patients by massaging the painful area with a solution of equal parts olive oil and eucalyptus oil, and having them eat a raw clove of garlic daily.

SINUS . . . Nosedrops to Shock Your System

Garlic/parsley tablets—2 every 4 hours (four or five times a day)—have been helpful in clearing up a chronic sinus condition.

This Russian remedy is dramatic and rather unpleasant, but considering the discomfort of a sinus condition and the super results reported from this remedy, it's worth doing. You may be able to say good-bye forever to that lingering or recurring sinus infection by following these instructions:

Put 2 medium-sized, peeled cloves of garlic through a garlic press into a small glass bowl. Mix it with 1 teaspoon distilled, spring, or filtered water. Let it settle so that the clear liquid is on top. Being careful not to suck in any of the garlic particles, fill an eyedropper with the clear liquid. At this point, you should enlist someone to help you. Keep your head back and have your assistant put 10 drops of the clear liquid into each nostril. Sniff. Hold your nostrils closed with your fingers, preventing the liquid from pouring out. After a couple of minutes, let the liquid run out into a tissue or simply blow your nose.

In reporting on this remedy, herbalist Jeanne Rose warns you, "prepare yourself for a shock." She recounts her experience of it, "My first feeling was one of intense burning in my upper nostrils. This feeling lasted for a few seconds. Then a brilliant red light burst inside my head, my eyes watered, and every opening of my body started sweating. Then I sniffed again, blew my nose, and everything returned to normal."

Doing this daily, Jeanne's sinuses cleared in 4 days, and her sense of smell returned in a week. After having severe recurrent sinus infections every 6 months for years, she has not been troubled with any since using this remedy. (Also see ALLERGIES, including Carlson Wade's Allergy-Ease Tonic.)

SLEEPLESSNESS (See INSOMNIA.)

SNEEZING . . . Keeping You Out of the Record Books

The Guinness Book of World Records, under "medical extremes," lists a young woman who sneezed for 978 days. During the first year, she sneezed an estimated 1 million times. The book neglects to report what stopped her close-to-three-years' sneezing fit, but we wouldn't be surprised to learn that it was garlic.

Medical research writer Rex Adams has two reports of continuous sneezers. In both cases, after the patients ate garlic, the sneezing seizures gradually subsided, then finally stopped.

It doesn't happen often, or to many people, but for those few achooers, chewing raw garlic may stop the spasms.

SORE THROAT . . . The Cause and the Cure

Remember, garlic is a great antibiotic, and since most sore throats are throat *infections*, be sure to eat 2 or more raw cloves a day and/or take garlic supplements—3 capsules twice a day with meals—until you're symptom free. (See Preparations chapter for Garlic Oxymel Syrup as a gargle.)

Make-Believe Candy

Peel a clove of garlic and pretend it's a sucking candy. Yes, suck on the clove of garlic. If you don't score it with your teeth, in other words, if you don't bite into it, it will be tolerable *and* effective in helping to clear up the problem. After a couple of hours, peel another clove and replace the old one with it.

Laryngitis

Garlic syrup is soothing and can help the voice come back to normal, especially when laryngitis is the end of a cold that settled in the throat and is accompanied by chest congestion. Take 1 teaspoon of the syrup every hour or two.

You may also find relief from drinking garlic tea throughout the day. (See Preparations chapter for Syrup and Tea)

Tonsillitis

GARLIC-SAGE TEA

Start with 1 quart of water in a glass, enamel, or porcelain pot, and add 1 tablespoon of garlic juice (some health food stores have bottled garlic juice, or you can juice cloves in a centrifugal juice extractor), plus 2 ounces of dried sage. Cover the pot and bring the mixture to a boil. As soon as it starts to boil, turn off the heat and let it stand until it's lukewarm. Strain the solution.

Drink 1/2 cup of this garlic-sage tea every 2 hours. Prepare another quart of the tea and gargle 1/2 cup (warming it each time) every hour until the condition is better.

STRESS (See NERVOUS TENSION.)

STROKE PREVENTION . . . An Excellent Daily Elixir

Noted medical anthropologist and author John Heinerman, Ph.D., in his book *The Healing Benefits of Garlic*, reported that many forms of garlic, including garlic oil, pills, syrup, tablets, tincture, vinegar, and wine are all helpful in stroke prevention. The one Dr. Heinerman likes best is the following recipe he created:

> "In a medium saucepan, combine one large head of garlic, separated into cloves and peeled, with 2 cups chicken or vegetable broth. Boil, then reduce to simmer for 15 minutes. Put the mixture with 2 bunches of parsley into a blender and purée. Season with kelp and drink daily."

(Also see HEART, BLOOD PRESSURE, and CHOLESTEROL.)

SUNBURN, WINDBURN . . . Take Tea and See

Take refrigerated garlic tea (see Preparations chapter), dip a white washcloth in it, wring it out, and place it on the sunburned or windburned area. (You'll probably need more than one washcloth to cover all the affected skin.) Be sure to protect your eyes before using this garlic tea compress on your face.

As soon as the cloth is no cooler than your body, redip, rewring, and reapply.

THRUSH (Oral Candida) . . . Thrash Thrush in a Rush

This yeast infection of the mouth, prevalent among children, can clear up quickly with garlic . . . a lot of garlic. For children with severe cases, use 1/4 to 1/2 teaspoon of garlic oil (see Preparations chapter) every couple of hours; for less severe cases, three to five times a day. For adults with severe cases, have up to 10 cloves of garlic in some form—raw, oil, syrup, capsules, and so on. The coated tongue should start clearing up within 24 hours after having garlic.

TOENAIL FUNGUS . . .
Nail the Problem With an Anti-Fungal Drink

This condition is quite common and not only limited to toenails. A fungal infection where the nail becomes thick and peculiar and discolors—turns brown or white—can also affect fingernails. This solution may be the solution:

In a saucepan, bring 1 cup water to a boil. Add 2 teaspoons powdered echinacea root (available at health food stores), and simmer for 10 to 15 minutes. Add a dozen minced garlic cloves and remove from heat. Steep for about 15 minutes. Strain. Add honey and lemon to taste. Drink cool or reheat. Drink this daily (right after a meal), until a new nail grows in completely. If the fungal infection is on the nail of the big toe, be patient. It may take a few months.

CAUTION: Check with your health professional before using this formula, especially if you're pregnant or over 65.

If the drink gives you a tingling sensation on your tongue, don't be alarmed. It's because of the echinacea, and it's normal and safe.

If the drink is too strong, dilute it with water. (Also see Athlete's Foot under FEET.)

TOOTHACHE . . . Ease the Pain; Fight the Infection

PLEASE NOTE: The following remedies do not take the place of a dentist's professional care. They may ease the pain of a toothache and help fight infection until you get to the dentist.

Place a peeled whole (uncut) clove of garlic directly on the aching tooth. Keep it there for a minimum of one hour. If the garlic is going to be touching the gum, you may want to first wrap it in a little piece of cheesecloth to protect sensitive gum tissue.

Also take garlic for its antibiotic properties, especially when a tooth is abscessed (see Preparations chapter for the Enhanced Garlic Formula under Nature's Amazing Antibiotic).

If you'd rather not put a garlic clove on your tooth, this remedy may be for you: Peel and mince 2 garlic cloves, wrap each minced clove in a piece of cheesecloth or muslin, and place them in the bend of each arm. Leave them there until the toothache subsides.

VAGINAL ITCHING . . . Douche Away Discomfort

Wash the genital area with garlic water (see Preparations chapter) and then douche with it. Follow that with a douche using 2 to 3 tablespoons of apple cider vinegar to 1 quart of water to restore the proper balance of vaginal bacteria.

WARTS . . . A *Twilight Zone* Treatment That Works

We've been researching and reporting folk remedies for well over a decade, and the most outrageous and successful remedies are the ones to ward off warts. Since you can't argue with success, here's one of them:

During the next full moon, at midnight, squeeze a clove of garlic through a press so that you have garlic juice and massage the juice on the wart. After several applications, expose the wart to direct moonlight in open air for 3 minutes. During that time, tell yourself that you will no longer nurture the wart. It will now wither and die.

This remedy, we are told, works especially well for children. During the 3-minute exposure to direct moonlight in open air, have them say:

Nasty wart, go away!
Part from me.
And do not stay.
Nasty wart, go away!

If the above remedy is too outrageous for you, then cut a clove of garlic in half and apply the juicy cut side of the clove on the wart, securing it in place with a bandage. Use 2 halves each day—one in the morning and the other at night—until the wart disintegrates. The average wart-disappearing time is a week.

Plantar Warts

At bedtime each night, take 1 or 2 garlic pearles (soft gels), puncture them and squeeze out the oil on the plantar warts. Do a thorough job of massaging the oil on the whole area for a few minutes. After you've let it set for a few more minutes, put a clean white sock on your foot and leave it on while you sleep. Give it a week or two for the little black roots to come out and fall off.

WEIGHT CONTROL . . . A Stop-the Craving Cocktail

Medical reporter Carlson Wade recommends that you:

> Begin your meal with a glass of salt-free vegetable juice, together with a mashed or diced garlic clove. It gives you speedy hunger satisfaction, and you will be satisfied with much smaller portions. Or take one of these garlic/vegetable juice cocktails to soothe your appetite between meals. In moments, your hunger pangs are eased. The grumblings are ended. Your eating urges are under control.
>
> The complex carbohydrates of the vegetable juice are stimulated by the garlic's gastroenteric allichalon to give you a sedative action by delaying excessive motor activity of your stomach.

WORMS (Intestinal Parasites, Vermifuge) . . . Test, Treatment, Prevention

John Lust, N.D., and author of *The Herb Book*, says, "Garlic is good for all kinds of worms and most other parasites as well."

According to Dian Dincin Buchman, Ph.D., investigator of natural medicine, "Almost every folk medicine notes the use of garlic to cleanse the entire system internally and help make the blood healthy while eliminating any poisonous bacteria, toxins, or worms."

A *Test for Worms*

Rectal itching, frequently a sign of worms, may make you aware that there is a problem. Dr. Buchman explains a way to find out if you have worms: "Attach transparent tape in the rectal fissure—it will *catch* the worms like fly paper. This does not cure the condition; it is only a diagnostic tool."

Just about all forms of garlic, including garlic oil, garlic water, a garlic enema (all found in Preparations chapter), and garlic supplements, will help rid you of intestinal parasites. A clove of garlic can even be used effectively as a suppository. Coat a peeled garlic clove with olive oil and insert it directly into the rectum each evening.

In the morning, before drinking or eating anything, peel and finely mince a medium-sized clove of garlic. Place it in a tablespoon and add a teaspoon of olive oil to it. Swallow it down. This is the hard part: Don't drink or eat anything until you've moved your bowels. Repeat the same procedure next morning. Try the transparent tape test (above), and if the tape is not all clear, then repeat the remedy on what would be the third morning.

Prevention

When traveling to primitive areas, particularly warm, windy climates with animals around (we hate to be the ones to tell you this, but—) chances are, under those conditions, intestinal parasites are airborne. The good news is, parasites that you inhale can be killed off before they can take hold if you eat garlic daily.

WOUNDS . . . The Fastest and Finest First Aid

It is well known and documented that British Army doctors used raw garlic cloves topically to control wound infections in World War I. Actually, for centuries, garlic has been used on wounds to help prevent infection or to treat infection that may have set in. Why stop now?

Most wounds require emergency measures, and your course of action will probably be determined by the form of garlic available to you at the time. Here are suggestions:

Clean the wound with garlic tea or garlic water (see Preparations chapter) or any other antiseptic that's within reach. Then sprinkle the wound with garlic powder and cover it with a dressing.

Or put a garlic poultice (also in Preparations chapter) on the wound. Clean the wound with an antiseptic each time you change the dressing, which should be at least a couple of times a day.

Anna Maria Clement, co-director of Hippocrates Health Institute in West Palm Beach, Florida, has been using garlic to heal open wounds of all kinds for the last 25 years, during the time she ran the Brandal Health Clinic in Sweden, and now at Hippocrates. Anna Maria says that pressed garlic is too strong to be the sole ingredient to put directly on the wound because it would burn the skin.

At the Institute, garlic is put through a press, then mixed with cold-pressed olive, canola, or flaxseed oil. Whichever oil you choose to use, it's important that it be *cold pressed*. The ratio of the mixture is one-third pressed garlic to two-thirds cold-pressed oil. Let it sit for 10 to 15 minutes, then dip gauze into the mixture and put the gauze on the open wound. Keep the mixture in a screwtop glass jar and refrigerate it. It will stay fresh up to 3 days.

"Recently," Anna Maria recalls, "a woman came to the Institute with an open ulcer after surgery. Her doctor said that it would take 6 weeks to heal. We treated it with the garlic mixture and it was fine in 2 days."

Brian Clement, director of Hippocrates, added that it's common for elderly people to arrive at the Institute with gaping wounds that they've had for years, and within a short time, thanks to garlic, the wounds are completely healed. (Also see INFECTIONS.)

YEAST INFECTION . . .
Symptoms and Suggestions for Men As Well As Women

The most common yeast infection, candidiasis, is caused by a yeastlike fungus called *Candida albicans* or *Monilia*.

William G. Crook, M.D., author of the revolutionary book *The Yeast Connection, A Medical Breakthrough*, says that 75 percent of his patients with this problem are women. "Yet, men, too, develop yeast-connected problems." The doctor particularly suspects such problems in men who:

- Are troubled by food and inhaled allergies
- Have been bothered by persistent jock itch, athlete's foot, or fungus infection of the nails
- Have taken repeated courses of antibiotics
- Consume lots of beer, breads, and sweets
- Crave alcohol
- Have wives or children bothered by yeast-connected illnesses
- Feel bad on damp days or on exposure to chemicals and/or tobacco
- Have an impaired sex drive
- Are troubled by fatigue, depression, and other peculiar nervous system symptoms
- Are bothered by recurrent digestive problems, including constipation, bloating, diarrhea, and abdominal pain

Daily doses of garlic—raw or supplements—can go a long way in helping prevent yeast infections.

Elaine Gillaspie, naturopathic physician, believes, "Nothing prevents yeast overgrowth as well as garlic does."

Michael T. Murray, N.D., and author of *Natural Alternatives to Over-the-Counter Drugs*, says

Garlic is especially active against *Candida albicans*, being more potent than nystatin, gentian violet, and six other reputed antifungal agents.

Dr. Crook urges his candidiasis patients to try garlic because it is a highly effective antifungal agent, in addition to having other health-promoting effects. He does however, offer a valid word of caution:

> Anything you eat or drink can cause an allergic reaction—especially if you consume it every day. If you're like most folks with a yeast-connected health problem, you're apt to be troubled by food sensitivities, and as good as garlic is for most people, it can cause allergic reactions.

Ann Louise Gittleman, M.S., C.N.S., author of *Guess What Came to Dinner*, says:

> Garlic is effective in killing parasites. Parasites may often be the underlying cause of the yeast problem in the first place.

For many, garlic can be a tremendous help, but if you have been troubled by frequently-recurring yeast infections, or one that just doesn't seem to go away completely, chances are you need more than garlic. You need a program that will pinpoint your food sensitivities and a daily diet that will strengthen your immune system while discouraging the growth of yeast. Dr. Crook's book and its companion cookbook written with Marjorie Hurt Jones, R.N., can be a good guide for helping you get control of an out-of-control yeast problem.

Garlic Remedies for Your Pet

DOSAGE

To determine the amount of an internal dose of garlic, consider the animal's body weight. It's always advisable to check with your animal's veterinarian.

According to Dr. Richard H. Pitcairn, the animal should get anywhere from 1/2 clove to 3 cloves of garlic depending on its size.

A small bird would get 1 or 2 drops of garlic oil. For an animal the size of a horse, the dosage might be double that for a large man.

With large animals, you can add garlic powder to the feed or chop the garlic cloves and mix it in with your pet's favorite food. To be sure that your pet eats all of the garlic, serve him a smaller amount of food than usual. Some pet owners get their furry friends to lap up raw garlic by finely mincing it into milk.

Whenever available, we report specific garlic dosages for remedies. Even so, be sure to keep in mind your pet's size and administer accordingly.

APPETITE RESTORER (Horses)

To perk up a horse's appetite, cut a clove of garlic in half and rub his teeth with the juicy sides of both halves. This folk remedy has been passed down for generations until it finally reached us. But we can't vouch for it because, well, we didn't get it straight from the horse's mouth.

ARTHRITIS

Veterinarian Richard H. Pitcairn recommends garlic for arthritic animals. He says that the herb—1/2 to 3 grated cloves, depending on the animal's size—is suited for the overweight animal with hip pain and is especially useful for one that has been on a high-meat diet.

BIRD MITES

A light sprinkling of garlic powder on birds can help prevent mites or other feather problems.

CANCER

Right now, in laboratories all over the world, scientific researchers are conducting tests using garlic on animals with cancer. Results have been promising, and extensive research and testing continue in the hope of finding a cure for cancer in humans. Meanwhile, after reviewing research papers, we've seen convincing evidence that garlic may boost the immune system, reduce the size of tumors, inhibit the growth of cancer cells, and more, for the prevention and treatment of different types of cancer. If garlic can improve the condition of terminal laboratory animals, it may also prove very beneficial to a sick pet.

Garlic also seems to do a good job keeping the animal's system clean and helping to restore the balance of vitamins and minerals. Give your pet garlic pearles (soft gels) daily. Make sure he also gets lots of filtered, spring, or distilled water.

If your pet has been diagnosed with cancer, chances are a veterinarian is on the case. Discuss garlic therapy with him or her and hopefully you'll be guided to garlic.

CONSTIPATION (Horses)

Separate all the cloves from 3 bulbs of garlic. As you proceed, marvel at the beauty of the bulb's magnificent structure. (Marveling has nothing to do with the remedy and everything to do with the appreciation of this great gift that's available to us in abundance.) Drop the cloves in a pot of water, bring it to a boil, then let it cook for 7 to 10 minutes. Once it cools, slip the peel off the cloves and mix them with 3 cut-up carob pods. Divide it in half and feed it to your horse in 2 portions during the day.

COUGHS (Dogs)

Every 3 hours give your dog 1 or 2 garlic capsules (dosage depending on the dog's size) until the cough subsides.

COUGHS (Horses)

Chop and combine 2 bulbs of garlic and 2 carrots, and mix it into the horse's feed once a day.

DIET (Cats and Dogs)

Health-Giving Daily Meal for Cats and Dogs

Andi Brown, expert in animal nutrition, shares her recipe for Spot's Stew, named for her black-and-white longhair cat. When Andi adopted him, he had horrendous health problems (too numerous and unpleasant to mention). Four days after being on this stew, Spot started to show great improvement, and a few weeks later, still on the stew, he made a complete recovery.

SPOT'S STEW

Ingredients:
2 onions, chopped coarsely
3/4 head of garlic, cloves peeled and chopped
1 whole fryer chicken (smallish)
16 ounces brown rice
handful of broccoli, cut up
4 carrots
1 whole zucchini
1 whole yellow squash
handful of green beans
2 stalks of celery

2 to 3 tablespoons vegetable oil

*In a 10-quart stock pot (stainless steel, please) put 2 to 3
tablespoons of vegetable oil. Heat oil and then brown the
onion and garlic lightly. Add the chicken (bones, skin, and
all). Fill pot with water to cover chicken. Add brown rice,
vegetables, and more water to cover. Cook over a low to
low-medium heat for about 3 hours. After the stew has finished cooking, let it cool, then debone the chicken. Use an
electric hand mixer and mix the chicken, rice, and vegetables into a purée.*

*Using plastic-lock bags or small empty milk cartons,
package up meal-sized portions and immediately freeze
what you don't need. Seek your pet's advice for ideal meal
size. (Andi makes up enough food to last a month.)*

For dogs: Add 1 slice of whole grain bread to each meal.

*Andi also adds a blend of cold-pressed oils (Dream
Coat) to provide the essential fatty acids which are missing once these ingredients have been cooked, and a blend
of water-soluble vitamins (Anitra's Vita-Mineral Mix), also
missing from the cooked dish.*

HEATHER'S GARLICKY DOG BISCUITS

Heather Simpson's recipe for a healthy treat is from the
International Garlic Festival Cookbook by Caryl Simpson.
Heather suggests that during holidays, when you're making
cookies for friends and relatives, these are fun and different
to add as gifts for their pets.

Ingredients:
1 cup white flour
1 cup whole wheat flour
1/2 cup powdered milk
1/2 teaspoon salt
1/2 tablespoon liver powder (available at health food stores)
1 teaspoon brown sugar
6 tablespoons vegetable oil
1 egg, beaten
1/2 cup water
10 large garlic cloves, finely minced

Heat oven to 325 degrees. Combine dry ingredients. Mix and add oil and egg. Add water to make a stiff dough. Knead until pliable. Roll out on floured surface 1/4- to 1/2-inch thick. Cut out with cookie cutters or biscuit cutter. Use bone-, cat-, or people-shaped cutters. Bake for 20 to 25 minutes.

EAR MITES (Cats and Dogs)

To treat ear mites, or to prevent them, put a few drops of garlic oil in your pet's ears. A pinch or two of garlic powder in the ears will also work well.

ECZEMA (Cats and Dogs)

This troublesome skin condition may be a signal that there's congestion in the digestive tract. A daily internal dose of garlic and a nutritionally sound diet may help eliminate the cause. To treat the symptom externally, combine 2 tablespoons cottage cheese, 2 tablespoons corn oil, 1 teaspoon wheat germ oil. Puncture a garlic pearle (soft gel), then squeeze in the oil, and mix thoroughly. Once or twice a day, massage this mixture on the animal's affected area.

A Gypsy folk remedy recommends a 3-day fast, giving the animal only honey-sweetened water to drink. The water is said to flush the toxins out of the system. On the fourth day, the animal should begin eating, and crushed garlic should be added to its diet. The dose for the average cat is 2 cloves of garlic mixed with milk or wrapped in a piece of its favorite food.

The external treatment consists of grinding acorns into powder and dusting the animal's sore skin with it.

FLEAS, LICE, AND TICKS (Cats and Dogs)

Raw garlic in your pet's diet can be a very effective flea repellent. For a cat, 1/2 clove a day should suffice; for a dog, 1/2 to 2 cloves a day, depending on the dog's size.

Brewer's yeast (available at health food stores) taken daily is said to enhance the effectiveness of garlic as a flea repellent. Give a cat 1 teaspoon of brewer's yeast daily, and 1 to 3 tablespoons for a dog, depending on its size.

A pet owner who rubs vegetable oil on his dog's skin, then massages in some garlic powder, says that his dog stays flea-free for a couple of months at a time.

INFECTIONS (Cats and Dogs)

The antibiotic formulas (see Preparations chapter) can be used internally and externally—best is both at the same time—when your pet has an internal or external infection.

INSECT BITES (Cats and Dogs)

Prepare this solution in advance: Peel and crush a clove of garlic and put it in a small jar with 1/2 cup white vinegar or lemon juice. Let it stay that way for a day, then refrigerate. Whenever your dog or cat gets an insect or spider bite, dip a cotton ball in the preparation and dab it on the bite.

INTESTINAL PARASITES (See WORMS.)

JAUNDICE (Cats and Dogs)

There are two types of jaundice: the type associated with liver disease and the other caused by the rapid breakdown of red blood cells, resulting in a backup of pigment which stains the tissues yellow. The latter noninflammatory simple jaundice can be treated by exposing your pet to direct or indirect sunlight for several hours a day for a few days. The inflamed-liver jaundice can be treated with a water fast for about 3 or 4 days. In addition to filtered, spring, or distilled water, each day the animal should be given garlic pearles (soft gels).

Consult your pet's veterinarian for a proper diagnosis and for treatment approval and dosage.

MANGE (Cats and Dogs)

This condition is caused by the *itch mite*, and it can be transmitted from dog to human or vice versa. (In humans the condition is called *scabies*.) The animal's symptoms are intense itching, irritation, and thickening of the skin. A human symptom is also intense itching, especially at night, wherever the animal made contact with the person.

Combine 1/4 cup olive oil with 2 tablespoons garlic powder and 2 tablespoons goldenseal powder. Mix thoroughly, then dab it often on your pet's affected area until it clears up.

As for you, the animal mange mite can live in human skin, but it cannot reproduce there. So eventually your problem will end on its own, unless reinfection occurs. Wear disposable rubber gloves when you touch your *mangy* dog.

SPIDER BITES (See INSECT BITES.)

TONIC (Cats and Dogs)

Use this tonic for its power to restore and invigorate your pet's entire system: In a screwtop jar combine 1 pint white vinegar, 2 tablespoons garlic powder, 4 tablespoons cod-liver oil, 5 tablespoons desiccated liver powder, and 4 tablespoons bone meal powder. (Desiccated liver and bone meal are available at health food stores.) Shake vigorously, then refrigerate. Every day, mix 3 tablespoons into your pet's food.

WORMS (Cats and Dogs)

Pinworms? Garlic. Tapeworms? Garlic. Roundworms? Garlic. Whipworms? Garlic. Hookworms? Garlic. Give your pet a substantial daily dose of raw chopped or grated garlic (see DOSAGE at the beginning of this chapter) and worms will be history.

Health-Giving Garlic Preparations

Wherever I found garlic in use, I found health.
Conversely, wherever I found healthy people, I found
that they were garlic eaters.

—Maurice Messegue
Way to Natural Health and Beauty, 1972

NATURE'S AMAZING ANTIBIOTIC

Throughout the Remedies chapter, reference is made to Lalitha Thomas's Enhanced Garlic Formula. Garlic is the number-one herbal antibiotic for any internal or external use. This formula doubles, or even triples, the strength and effectiveness of garlic alone, while it helps the body to more quickly assimilate the garlic and thus put it to work. Chances are, when an antibiotic action is required, you will not have to use anything else besides plain garlic or this formula.

It is with great appreciation to this extraordinary herbalist that we present it here for you:

ENHANCED GARLIC FORMULA

Ingredients:

1 part garlic powder (bought in bulk at an herb store)

1/4 part cayenne powder

1 part powdered calcium ascorbate (a form of vitamin C that's
   available at health food stores and has a potency of 1/4 teaspoon = 1 gram of vitamin C)

Depending on the amount of the formula you intend to
make, 1 part can equal: 1 pinch, 1 ounce, 1 tablespoon,
and so on.

If you prefer, you can mix only the garlic and cayenne
together as powders and take 1 gram of vitamin C (calci-
um ascorbate) in tablet form with each dose or as needed.

It's advisable to make a large enough quantity so you always have extra on hand for emergency use. Store in an airtight container in a cool, dry place for best shelf life.

If you are not getting the results you want from this formula, you may have a tough-case "germ" that calls for an additional antibiotic herb, as in the following:

ALTERNATIVE ANTIBIOTIC FORMULA

Mix together equal parts of chaparral, garlic, and slippery elm powders for internal and external use.

Dosage for children 4 to 10 years: *1/4 to 1/2 teaspoon in water, as often as every 2 hours, up to eight times a day, depending upon the seriousness of the condition.*

Dosage for children 11 years to adults: *1/2 to 1 teaspoon in water, as often as every 2 hours, up to eight times a day, depending upon the seriousness of the condition.*

When using garlic as an antibiotic, always drink at least 2 quarts of pure (distilled) water and/or herb tea during the day to help flush toxins out of your body.

GARLIC BATHS FOR RESTORING HEALTH

Yes, a garlic bath! It's a great preventive measure, especially during flu season. No, your skin won't reek of garlic, just don't wet your hair in the bath water.

If you are more ambitious, you can peel the cloves of 3 to 4 bulbs of garlic (or more) and tie them in a piece of cheesecloth. Place the resulting bundle of garlic in a large pot of boiling water, cover and steep for at least an hour. Then pour the garlic water into the bathtub, drop in the bundle of garlic, too, then add warm water.

Garlic baths can be very beneficial for ailments such as colds, muscular aches and pains, bladder and urinary problems, and fever.

COMPRESS (See TEA and VINEGAR AND GARLIC.)

ENEMA . . . Nature's Special Cleanser

Enemas, one of the greatest herbal cleansers, help shorten the recovery period, particularly for colds and stomach flu, constipation, amebic dysentery, parasites, and mononucleosis.

Fill an enema bag with 2 quarts of tepid garlic water (see Garlic Water on p. 108). If this is your first enema, it will be a learn-by-doing experience. As you get into it, you will discover what works best for you in your bathroom.

Spread a towel on the floor of the bathroom so that you don't lie down on cold tile. Hang the apparatus a couple of feet above the floor. You may have to put up a clothing hook or rig something with a hanger and the door knob or shower curtain rod.

Put petroleum jelly or olive oil on the tip of the enema, then gently insert it into your rectum as you lie on your left side. Let the water flow in slowly. When the enema bag is about half empty, rotate onto your back, then slowly to your right side, so that the water fills the lower intestines. The average adult should be able to hold 2 quarts of garlic water in the colon. Hold it for as long as possible.

After an Enema

During the next few days following each enema, it's a good idea to take acidophilus (available at health food stores), and/or to eat plain (nonfat) yogurt (make sure it contains live active culture) to help get your system back in balance.

FOOTBATH . . . For a Treatment and a Treat

Treat yourself to Lalitha's Footbath. According to the renowned herbalist, the footbath will draw toxins from the entire body, soothe tension and anxiety, rejuvenate sore or tired feet and legs, help treat athlete's foot (also see Athlete's Foot in FEET in Remedies chapter), speed recovery from colds and flu, relieve toxic buildup from a daily job environment that may be physically or emotionally polluted or stressful, and much, much more. And, it feels so good.

In keeping with our method and Lalitha's formula, you'll need 2 plastic shoe boxes. They're easy to get, inexpensive, neat, and a very convenient, comfortable way way to bathe one's feet. Each shoe box holds about 2 quarts of water, allowing for the amount displaced by the foot. To soak both feet, you'll need a gallon of water—distilled, spring, or filtered (the purer, the better). Take 10 to 16 cloves of fresh garlic and crush well or put them in a blender with 2 cups of the pure water. Then divide the crushed garlic evenly into the 2 shoe boxes, and do the same with the rest of the gallon of water. (If you prefer to use a large basin, that's good, too.) Now you're ready to soak your feet. You may want to get something good to read, or lower the lights and turn on soothing music . . . whatever quiets your soul, as your soles soak for at least 20 minutes.

GARLIC WATER . . .
Combining Nature's Two Miraculous Healers

Garlic water is made from fresh garlic crushed or blended well in pure (distilled) water. Strain out the pulp, or not, according to use. This water can be added to a footbath, bathtub, enema bag, or used as an antibiotic wash for wounds, as a spray for plant diseases, or as a plant insect repellent.

For internal use such as an enema, begin with a mild mixture, using 1 (generally for babies) or 2 cloves of garlic for each quart of water. For external use such as a footbath, it is fine to have a stronger mixture, such as 1 garlic clove for each cup of water. To make a large amount of garlic water, it is often simplest to first make a concentrate by blending many cloves of garlic with 2 or 3 cups of water. Then dilute this mixture to the strength desired.

If you plan to put the garlic water through a sprayer, enema tube, and so on, you must first strain it well to prevent small garlic bits from plugging up any equipment.

JUICE . . . A Potent Potable

You can put garlic cloves through a juicer, just be aware that even after you thoroughly clean the juicer, whatever gets juiced the next several times after using garlic will taste of garlic. If that's objectionable, use a garlic press to get the juice you need. Or, check your local health food store for a bottle of garlic juice. Also check our Resources chapter.

If you're into juicing, or want to get into it, here's a wonderful *juiced* health drink:

GARLIC EXPRESS

from *Juicing for Life* by Cherie Calbom and Maureen Keane (Avery Publishing Group, 1992)

For:
Shoring up the immune system
Easing depression
Hypertension
Stress
Subduing salt cravings
Subduing peanut butter cravings

Ingredients:
Handful parsley
1 garlic clove
4–5 carrots, greens removed
2 stalks celery

Bunch up parsley and push through a centrifugal juice extractor with garlic, carrots, and celery.

"Juices rich in the antioxidant nutrients beta-carotene and vitamin C strengthen the immune system," says co-author Cherie Calbom, M.S., a certified nutritionist in Kirkland, Washington. "But because sugar—even fruit sugar—has been shown to depress the immune system, I tell people to get their vitamins from vegetable juices rather than from fruit juices, especially when they're fighting infections."

LINIMENT (See WASH AND LINIMENT.)

LOZENGES (See GARLIC OXYMEL SYRUP.)

OIL . . . A Versatile Internal/External Healing Blend

Botanical researcher-herbalist, Paul Schulick, who is president of New Chapter, Inc. (see Resources chapter) shares his recipe for garlic oil:

GARLIC OIL

Into 16 ounces of extra virgin olive oil, blend 1 fresh whole peeled bulb of garlic, approximately 15 cloves. Blend until milky and store in refrigerator. This should be a 2-week supply. After 2 weeks, make a fresh batch of this olive oil maceration.

Aside from the many medicinal uses of garlic oil, this recipe is excellent to use as a base oil for stir-frying.

WARNING: Homemade preparations containing *garlic-in-oil* must be refrigerated. Do not keep it longer than 2 weeks.

The University of California at Berkeley *Wellness Letter* explains:

If not handled properly, garlic-in-oil preparations carry the risk of botulism. Garlic can pick up the bacterium that causes botulism from the soil in which it grows; then once the garlic in oil is covered, spores will have an ideal oxygen-free environment in which to germinate. The resulting toxin cannot be detected by taste or smell.

Commercial garlic-in-oil products are safe when they contain an antibacterial or acidifying agent, such as phosphoric or citric acid. Those that do not contain such ingredients, and thus require refrigeration, have been banned by the FDA.

REMEMBER: Refrigerate all garlic-in-oil preparations! It's a good idea to label them with the date. Do not store them longer than 2 weeks.

Foot Massage With Garlic Oil

"Foot massage is my favorite way to bring healing herbs into the body," says Paul Schulick. "It combines loving touch with the benefits of reflexology and transdermal (through or by way of the skin) delivery. Transdermal garlic is so valuable because it avoids the potential irritation to the gastric mucosa (stomach lining) and ensures the highest blood levels of valuable garlic constituents. Olive oil is a perfect transdermal carrier because it is rich in oleic acid, a proven transdermal penetrator.

With the protection of plastic undercoat and a cotton cloth, massage the garlic oil liberally into feet for a minimum of 20 minutes. This is a perfect treatment for colds and flu, and as part of a regenerative program for people who are suffering from chronic illness."

POULTICE . . . A Remedy for Remarkable Results

Use a poultice to draw out infection and break up congestion anywhere in the body, internally as well as externally (except the eyes). It also can provide antibiotic action right through the skin to where it's needed.

Before applying a raw garlic poultice directly on the skin, test for sensitivity with the juicy side of a half clove garlic on a very small patch of skin. If, after a few minutes, the skin turns red and seems irritated or about to blister, apply a thin layer of oil (castor oil, vitamin E oil, olive oil) or petroleum jelly, then apply crushed garlic (the amount depends on the size of the affected area) in cheesecloth or gauze, keeping it in place with tape or a bandage. Put a hot, wet towel over it to keep it warm and moist.

GARLIC/MISO SUPER SOUP

from Annemarie Colbin, certified health education specialist, *Food and Healing* (Ballantine Books, 1996):

> *For that under-the-weather, about-to-come-down-with-something feeling. Also helpful in overcoming the effects of antibiotics, particularly when taken with 2 acidophilus*

capsules a day (available at health food stores) for a few days to a week after a course of conventional antibiotics.

Ingredients:
1 quart water or stock
1 whole head garlic, cloves separated and peeled
1 heaping tablespoon miso, or to taste (available at health food stores)

Simmer the garlic cloves in the water or stock for 15 minutes; fish them out and put them in the blender with a little stock and the miso; puree, return to pot with the rest of the stock, adjust taste, and serve hot.

SOOTHING GARLIC SYRUPS

COLD AND COUGH SYRUPS

from Lelord Kordel, health and nutrition researcher

Ingredients:
1 tablespoon peeled, chopped garlic
1/2 cup honey
1 teaspoon horseradish (fresh, scraped root is preferred; if not available, use prepared)

Mix well and take 1 or 2 tablespoons as needed. If mixture is too hot, add more honey to taste.

COUGH SYRUP

from *The Stinking Rose Cookbook*

Ingredients for 1-1/2 quarts:
1 pound peeled and sliced garlic cloves
3 tablespoons braised fennel seeds
3 tablespoons caraway seeds
vinegar
sugar

Place garlic in a large pot with 1 quart of cold water. Bring to a boil and cook until garlic is soft. Add fennel and caraway seeds. Cover and let stand for 12 hours. Strain the liquid and add an equal amount of vinegar. Bring to a boil and add enough sugar to make a syrup. When a cough acts up, take 2 to 3 tablespoons.

GARLIC OXYMEL SYRUP

According to Debra St. Claire, master herbalist, an *oxymel* is used to disguise the taste of unpleasant herbs. Her Garlic Oxymel Syrup can be used as a gargle for a sore throat, as cough syrup, as the basis for lozenges, and as a daily preventive tonic.

Ingredients:
4 ounces freshly sliced garlic
1 pint raw apple cider vinegar
20 ounces honey (raw is best)

For lozenges, you'll also need:
1 cup slippery elm powder
essential oil to taste, such as peppermint or spearmint

Equipment:
1-quart saucepan
cheesecloth
large mixing bowl
wooden spoon
candy thermometer
large strainer
straining cloth
rubber gloves
1 pint amber storage bottle
label

Procedure:

Slice the garlic. Pour the vinegar in the saucepan, stir in the garlic and bring to a boil, then reduce to simmer for 5 minutes (tightly covered). Strain and press out the garlic (rubber gloves are helpful here, it's hot!), then return the liquid to the pan and stir in the honey. Simmer down, on medium-high (uncovered), until the mixture reaches the consistency of thick syrup. On a candy thermometer, the temperature should read approximately 200 degrees. At this point, you can decant the syrup into an amber glass jar or turn all of it or a portion of it into lozenges (instructions below).

Recommended dosage:

2 tablespoons a day as a tonic; as a cough syrup, a tablespoon whenever the cough acts up. For a sore throat, put 1 tablespoon in a glass of warm water and gargle every hour.

GARLIC OXYMEL LOZENGES

Put 1/2 cup of the Garlic Oxymel Syrup in a bowl and stir in enough slippery elm powder to make a dough. Mix in 1/2 ounce of the essential oil to taste. Work it in well, then roll out the dough and cut into lozenges, adding the slippery elm powder when necessary to keep it from getting sticky. Place the lozenges on a plate to dry, then store in an amber glass container away from heat and direct sunlight.

TEA . . . Decoction and Infusion

Of the many ways to prepare garlic tea, we've selected the three we consider simple and effective. These suggestions hold true for all:

- Use the purest water possible—distilled, spring, or filtered.
- Prepare tea in a glass, enamel, or porcelain pan. Do not use aluminum or cast iron.

- These preparations are strong. Drink 1/2 cup (or less) at a time, and not many cups throughout the day. *More* is not always better, nor is *stronger* always better.
- Sip slowly.
- Leftover tea may be refrigerated, then reheated to tepid to drink.
- Tea may be used as a hot or cold compress.

INSTANT POWDERED GARLIC TEA

Add 1/4 teaspoon of garlic powder (preferably bought in bulk at an herb store) to a cup of water that just started to bubble, not boil. When cool enough to drink, sip slowly.

GARLIC DECOCTION

(a concentrated herbal tea made by simmering)

For each 1/2 teaspoon chopped garlic clove, use 2-1/2 cups water. Put the garlic and water in a pan and simmer on lowest fire, covered, for 15 minutes. Take off heat, keep covered, and let cool to room temperature. Strain and drink.

This decoction acts as an excellent decongestant, especially for asthmatics.

GARLIC INFUSION

(a concentrated herbal tea made by steeping)

Between the simmering of a decoction and the steeping of an infusion, the latter is generally milder.

Crush or chop 1 to 3 garlic cloves. Put the garlic in a jar or pot that has a tight cover and can hold a pint of water. Add the pint of just-boiled water over the garlic, cover the container, and let it steep until it's room temperature. Strain and drink.

BRONCHITIS AND ASTHMA TEA

from Dee Poser, Northwest Garlic Festival

Ingredients:
4 cups chicken broth
1 bulb garlic (15 cloves) peeled and crushed
1 teaspoon cilantro
1 teaspoon parsley
1 teaspoon mint leaves
1 teaspoon sweet basil
1/2 teaspoon lemon pepper
1 teaspoon curry powder

Combine all ingredients in a glass or enamel pot. Bring to boil, then boil for 10 to 15 minutes. Heat 1/2 cup and drink before bedtime.

TONIC . . . To Wake Up "Tired Blood"

Carlson Wade recommends that you drink this Iron Tonic in the morning, preferably before breakfast. We think it may be a little irritating on an empty stomach. Our recommendation is that you drink it *after* breakfast or after eating a portion of nonfat yogurt.

IRON TONIC

from Carlson Wade

Ingredients:
2 garlic cloves
1 tablespoon wheat bran
2 tablespoons brewer's yeast
1/2 cup salt-free tomato juice
1/2 cup skim milk
1/4 cup prune juice

Blenderize all ingredients until thoroughly combined. The rich iron combines with the garlic and the other vitamins and minerals to sweep away the cobwebs from your bloodstream and give you a wide-awake look and feel, physically and mentally. It works in minutes! It lasts for days!

VINEGAR AND GARLIC . . . Skin Saver

Herbal practitioners use garlic vinegar as a cold compress on skin problems such as bed sores and wounds. It's also used to remove corns, calluses, and warts. Wet a cotton puff with garlic vinegar, tape it to the unwanted whatever, and leave it on overnight. Repeat the procedure in the morning (if convenient), and again at night until you get the desired result.

GARLIC VINEGAR

Crush one large garlic clove for each cup of red wine vinegar or apple cider vinegar you want to prepare. Put the appropriate amount of garlic in the bottle of vinegar and close tightly. Let it stay that way for 10 days. Then strain and use.

WASH AND LINIMENT . . . Internal/External Healer

ANTI-INFECTION WASH
AND ARTHRITIS PAIN LINIMENT

from Dian Dincin Buchman, Ph.D., author of *Herbal Medicine* (Wings Books)

Ingredients:
1 quart apple cider
4 ounces garlic juice (see JUICE)
1/2 ounce grated horseradish root

Add garlic and horseradish to the cider. Put the cider in a warm place for 12 hours. Shake the container often.

Then remove it to a cool place. Let it stand another 12 hours. Strain the liquid and place it in a labeled jar. Keep it in a cool place or refrigerate.

To fight infection, take a teaspoon at a time, internally, one to three times a day between meals, or externally on a cloth for a wound or painful joints. This is a stimulating wash for sore or stiff muscles, rheumatic, sciatic, or arthritic pain, and can be used to encourage circulation in some paralyzed parts. For sensitive skin, first apply an oil such as castor oil.

Growing Garlic

*Garlic has a genuine mystique some people would call
an actual "power." The plant's simplicity is fascinating and prehistoric. It's not difficult to imagine this
plant growing at the dawn of time.*

*Then there is the bulb, each bulb a clone of some
fantastically old mother-bulb that has grown,
regrown, and multiplied its original cells for millen-
nia. There are awesome traces of human history bun-
dled beneath the bulb wrappers, each wrapper like a
giant step through time toward the very origins of cultivated food-plants on our planet. Garlic bulbs don't
pass on their ancient memories—they are their
ancient memories.*

—Ron L. Engeland
Growing Great Garlic—The Definitive Guide
for Organic Gardeners and Small Farmers
(Filaree Productions)

According to organic farmer Ron Engeland, "The ideal environment for many varieties of garlic is one with moderately cold win-
ters, good snow cover, adequate fall and spring moisture, a warm
and dry June and July with good direct sunlight and low humidity,
and a light sandy loam with moderate organic matter and good
drainage. Moderate elevations of 2,000 to 4,000 feet can also be
helpful because they ensure cooler summer nights and they seldom experience excessively high summer temperatures."

If that doesn't describe your garden, take heart. Garlic is a
hardy herb that's grown successfully throughout the world.

Growing instructions vary greatly along with geographical
locations, climate, and soil conditions. The following garlic-
growing information is based on generalizations that should be
modified for your area of the country and the specific space and
soil in which you plan to plant.

WHEN TO PLANT

September, October, November—the main consideration to help
you know when to plant is that garlic needs to grow roots before

the freezing weather sets in. So if you plant about 4 to 6 weeks before the ground normally freezes, you will allow good root development, but not top-growth prior to winter.

The traditional day to plant garlic in the South is on Thanksgiving Day. In the North, the traditional garlic-planting day is Columbus Day, October 12.

According to practicing witch Gerina Dunwich, "Favorable results are always obtained when herbs are planted in harmony with Mother Nature. The phase of the moon and the sign of the zodiac the moon is in when the herb is planted are extremely important. Garlic should be planted during a new or half moon in the sign of Scorpio (October 23 to November 21) or Sagittarius (November 22 to December 21)."

Some say garlic should be planted on the shortest day of the year and harvested on the longest day of the year.

GROWING CONDITIONS

Garlic likes a sunny patch in a garden. Garlic also likes rich, well-drained soil. It doesn't do well in light or tight soils that lack organic matter and tilth. Sulfur and sulfides in the soil are said to increase the potency and flavor of the garlic. Heavy clay soil will cause irregular-shaped bulbs.

Keep soil evenly moist. Dry soil will result in irregular-shaped bulbs.

Apartment dwellers with terraces can grow garlic in a planter box that's at least 12 inches deep, 12 inches wide and a couple of feet long.

Apartment dwellers without terraces can grow green garlic (see below) in a window box or indoors.

GARLIC AS A COMPANION PLANT

- When garlic is planted around fruit and nut trees, it helps to repel moles.
- Garlic planted near roses, lettuce, and peas helps keep aphids away.

- If you have a bird problem, plant garlic throughout the garden and the birds will stay away.
- If you have a problem with Japanese beetles, plant garlic around the edges of your garden to repel them.
- Do not plant garlic where other onion family plants grew the year before because onions' pests, such as thrips, can be passed along to the garlic. You can plant garlic where potatoes grew the prior year, and the garlic will use any available nitrogen the potatoes did not use. Also, there are no crossover pests or pathogens from potatoes.

WHAT TO PLANT

Garlic is divided into two subspecies: *ophioscorodon* (referred to as "ophio," or "topsetting" or "hardneck" garlics), and *sativum* (referred to as "softneck" or "artichoke," or "Italian," or "Silverskin" garlics).

Yes, you can go to your neighborhood green grocer and buy a bulb and plant those cloves, and you may get a decent harvest, but it's very chancy. Put the odds in your favor by knowing which varieties of garlic grow best in your area and by buying bulbs from a reliable source. Is there an organic garlic farmer or nursery near you? In some cities, like New York, farmers come to town to sell their produce once a week at (schoolyard or parking lot) green markets. Those are good places to make contact with organic garlic farmers. Most serious gardeners buy bulbs from a reputable mail order seed house (see Resources chapter for Filaree Farm, with over 400 varieties—the largest garlic collection in the United States—with 100 varieties available by mail).

Garlic *cloves* are the *seeds*, and what you plant is what you get. Plant skinny little cloves, and you grow skinny little bulbs. Plant big, beautiful bruise-free cloves, and you know the rest.

Once you get the seedbulbs, you must break them into individual cloves—a process known as *clove popping* or *clove cracking*. Be especially careful when popping or cracking that you do not bruise the cloves in any way. Bruised cloves provide a suitable site for fungi and diseases.

Do not peel the cloves.

Plant cloves as soon as possible after popping—don't wait longer than a day or two. They're susceptible to mold, disease, and drying out.

HOW MUCH TO PLANT

According to the Filaree Farm catalogue: One pound of garlic yields about 3/4 pounds of large plantable cloves.

One to three pounds of planting stock should produce plenty of garlic for average gardening families. Garlic lovers may need two to three times as much. (Some families have no trouble eating 10 pounds of garlic per month.) Remember, softneck garlics store longer than many hardneck types.

You'll get 7 to 9 bulbs per pound of garlic that are, in size, 2 to 2-1/2 inches in diameter. Rocamboles average 4 to 6 large plantable cloves per bulb. Purple stripe bulbs are similar to Rocamboles in the number of plantable cloves. Porcelain and Asiatic bulbs average 4 to 6 cloves per bulb and all are usually plantable. Artichoke and Silverskin bulbs have more cloves per bulb and may average up to 8 large cloves per bulb.

For ballpark estimates in small areas of single rows with 4 inches between plants, figure about 6 pounds of hardneck bulbs per 100 feet, and 4 pounds of softneck bulbs per 100 feet.

PLANTING NATURE'S GIFT

Once you have your unbruised, firm, mold- and disease-free cloves that still have their skins on, plant them flat side down/point up. (The roots grow from the flat side.)

Depth of planting can be anywhere from 1 inch to 4 inches beneath the surface of the soil, the consideration being how severe the winter tends to be. The colder the winter, the deeper they're usually planted.

To decide the distance between each clove, organic farmer Ron Engeland says, "A basic rule of thumb is a distance twice the desired bulb diameter." If you're planting cloves from the average bulb that's 2-1/2 inches in diameter, plant one clove every 5 inches.

MULCHING . . . Mother Earth's Blanket

Farmer Engeland explains, "A good mulch moderates soil conditions. It will prevent outrageous excesses in temperature and moisture levels, and protect soil from extreme physical, chemical, and biological variations that may hinder or actually harm plants."

The farmer's favorite mulch is fresh grass clippings from his orchard. He has also used well-chopped deciduous (fallen) leaves.

FOUR IMPORTANT GROWING TIPS

- Keep garlic beds weed-free. A weedy garlic patch will result in small bulbs.
- Although garlic is used as an effective pesticide (see GARLIC PESTICIDE below), there are diseases to watch for, including Fusarium, a fungus that causes black spotting of the skin and rotting cloves, and nematodes (tiny soil worms). Insects to watch for include mites and cutworms.
- In spring when plants are growing green leaves, water like any garden green. Nitrogen is appreciated at this stage of growth.
- Garlic requires moisture throughout its growing period. Do not allow the plants to dry out completely. Once stalks begin to droop and turn brown, stop watering.

HARVESTING . . . Repeating the Rewards

Once the stalks get dry, turn yellow, and start to fall over, it's harvest time—generally, in late July or early August.

Instead of pulling out the garlic bulbs, dig them up with a garden fork. Don't be surprised when there isn't any papery skin around the bulbs. The skin, as you know it, happens during the curing process.

If you're harvesting on a hot, sunny day, do not leave the freshly dug bulbs in direct sunlight. Take them to a cool, dry place where there is air circulating.

CURING . . . Garlic's Coming of Age

To prevent mold, the relative humidity should be below 70 percent throughout the curing period. It may take up to a month for the moisture to evaporate, the flavor to strengthen, and the outer skin to become papery.

If you want to braid your harvest, do so while the tops still have moisture and are flexible, or at least not so dry that they cannot be re-wet before braiding.

Once they're thoroughly dry/cured, you can hang them in your kitchen; they're ready to be used. Or, once they're completely cured, the neck may be cut about 1/2-inch above the bulb. Store in netted bags. (See the Garlic As Food chapter for more storage tips.)

GARLIC GREENS . . . Vitality Sprouts

Master herbalist Debra St. Claire shares her growing instructions for garlic greens, based on the teachings of Edmond Bordeaux Szekely, Ph.D., who was a strong proponent of biogenic (life-sustaining) foods. Professor Szekely believed that by eating a plant in its *baby* stages, you will get the most vitality out of that plant. He suggested that instead of eating garlic cloves, you use the cloves to grow baby greens and eat those. Whenever Debra St. Claire feels a cold coming on, she eats a bunch of baby greens—and good-bye cold.

To grow garlic greens, use a planter that's at least 10 inches in diameter and 6 inches deep. Fill it with good organic soil. Take large, firm bulbs, carefully *crack* them (separate the cloves) without bruising the cloves, and leave the peel on. Then plant them, pointy side up, not any deeper than the length of the clove itself, and very close together (approximately an inch apart). You should be able to plant about 40 cloves.

Depending on the season, the little green shoots will appear in as few as 3 days. When the greens are about 6 to 8 inches tall, snip them off close to the soil, but don't pull out the plant. In this way, the green shoots will continue to grow and may be snipped off several times before the plant finally turns brown.

Eat them raw in salads, on sandwiches, or cook with them.

GARLIC PESTICIDE

The following solution is strong stuff! It can be irritating to skin and eyes. Wear goggles and rubber gloves when preparing it in your kitchen and using it in your garden.

Separate the cloves of 1 average garlic bulb and toss them into a blender along with 1 small onion, 2 tablespoons cayenne pepper, and 1 quart water. After blending, pour it into a container and let it steep for an hour. Then mix in 1 tablespoon unscented liquid soap (not detergent).

The solution can be stored in a tightly closed glass jar and refrigerated for about a week. Do not use this potent pesticide on seedlings. It is advisable to test all other plants before using. Try it on a few leaves and wait a day or two, then check the leaves for any adverse effects. If the leaves look fine, sprinkle it around, and don't forget your goggles and rubber gloves! (Also see the Resources chapter for an environmentally safe commercial insect repellent called Garlic Barrier.)

Garlic
As Food

PREPARATION TIPS

Garlic Varieties Available in the United States

- American garlic, which is most common, has a white, papery skin and is strongest in flavor.
- The purply-mauve-reddish varieties are somewhat milder than the white and come from any number of places, including Mexico, South America, Italy, and China.
- Elephant garlic is a sheep in wolf's cloves. It's really a form of leek, and it lacks the juicy pungency of true garlic. According to chef/restaurateur Bob Kinkead, "Elephant garlic has a much milder flavor and little of the same fragrant impact that inspires garlic lovers." Also, its staying power is not nearly as long as that of its smaller relatives.

Hints for Shopping for Garlic

- Buy bulbs that are sold loose, rather than packaged, so that you can see and feel them in order to make your selection.
- The papery, outer skin should be taut and unbroken.
- Beware of green shoots sprouting, discoloration, mold, rot (feel for soft spots), or shriveling. When garlic gets old, it dries out and begins to shrivel; its flavor dissipates and it becomes bitter.
- Keep in mind: plump, firm, compact, heavy for its size, solid.
- A bulb has anywhere from 8 to 40 cloves. Average is about 15 cloves. Look for bulbs with large cloves so you can cut down on peeling time.

Five Tips for Storing Garlic

- Store garlic bulbs away from any heat source, a stove, or the sun. A cool, dry, dark place is ideal, and in an open container, a crock with ventilation holes or a net bag that allows air to circulate around them. (See Resources chapter for commercial garlic keepers.)

- Storage time: Generally, unbroken bulbs can stay for a couple of months or more; once separated from the bulb, cloves should be used in less than 2 weeks. Exact storage time depends on the variety of garlic you have, its age when you bought it, and storage conditions.
- As for refrigerating garlic, many adamantly say NO! Larry D. Lawson, Ph.D., research scientist and one of the world's leading authorities on garlic, reasoned that when you buy garlic in the spring, most likely that garlic comes from last year's harvest and had to be kept somewhere (commercially) refrigerated.

After doing his own studies on refrigerating garlic, his conclusion is that there's no problem with it as long as you don't put the bulbs in a plastic bag. In fact, Dr. Lawson explained that the enzyme that converts the alliin's parent sulfur compound to alliin slowly becomes present when the bulb thinks winter is coming. The bottom line is, when you put the bulb in the refrigerator, gradually more alliin will be produced, which means you will eventually end up with more allicin (the compound many believe to be the great healer). The tradeoff is if you let it go too long in the fridge, it will sprout. Well, then you can eat the sprouts.

- Do not freeze uncooked garlic. Its consistency will break down and it will have an awful ungarlic smell.
- To store peeled cloves, place them in a jar and cover them with olive oil. Close the jar so that it's airtight and refrigerate. It will keep for about 2 weeks. When you've used up the cloves, you're left with garlic-flavored oil that can be used for sautéing, stir-frying, on salads, and brushed on bread.

WARNING: Homemade preparations containing garlic-in-oil (garlic-in-butter, salad dressing, marinade, etc.) must be refrigerated. Do not keep it longer than 2 weeks.

The University of California at Berkeley *Wellness Letter* explains:

> If not handled properly, garlic-in-oil preparations carry the risk of botulism. Garlic can pick up the bacterium that causes botulism from the soil in which it grows;

then once the garlic in oil is covered, spores will have an ideal oxygen-free environment in which to germinate. The resulting toxin cannot be detected by taste or smell.

"Commercial garlic-in-oil products are safe when they contain an antibacterial or acidifying agent, such as phosphoric or citric acid. Those that do not contain such ingredients, and thus require refrigeration, have been banned by the FDA.

REMEMBER: Refrigerate all garlic-in-oil preparations! It's a good idea to label them with the date. Do not store them longer than 2 weeks.

Cracking or Popping

- Either term—cracking or popping—is used by garlic growers when referring to separating cloves from the bulb. To crack or pop the bulb quickly and easily, place it pointy-side down on a hard surface, and with the palm of your hand—maybe both hands—press down on the bulb's root end. That should do it.
- Bob Kinkead offers a valuable word of caution: "Don't put lots of garlic skins in your garbage disposal. This helpful hint was gleaned from the experience of having my sink back up one Thanksgiving Day."

Peeling Garlic

- Place the flat side of a French, or chef's knife on top of a clove and gently pound the blade with the bottom of your fist, and the peel will crack open. If you want to crush the clove, put more power behind the pound. If you prefer not to use a knife and your fist, try a blunt object like the bottom of a pot or a bottle or a rolling pin.
- Drop cloves into boiling water and cook for about 40 seconds. (Keep them in boiling water for a few minutes and it will reduce the garlic's potency.) Transfer them to a colander, let cold water run over them, then peel when they're cool enough to touch.
- Microwave the cloves for 30 seconds.

- Dry-roast cloves in an open skillet until the skins start breaking open—it shouldn't take more than 2 minutes.
- If you peel cloves that you don't plan on using right away and you nick one, use that one as soon as possible or it will get moldy.
- There are several inexpensive commercial peelers on the market that make peeling garlic fast and fun. (See the Resources chapter for vendors of commercial peelers.)

Chopping Garlic

Bob Kinkead shares his good advice:

> Chopping garlic is one of those basic kitchen skills that actually requires a bit of precision because the cloves are relatively small, and they need to be finely diced to release all their flavor. Also, it's unpleasant to bite into a coarse chunk of raw garlic, and chunks don't sauté well. Coarsely chopped garlic burns before it can fully release its flavor, and the flavor of burned garlic can permeate an entire dish.
>
> The tool I don't recommend for chopping garlic is a food processor; the machine will knock the cloves around and nick them up, but it won't give you the fine chop that you need.
>
> It's easiest to chop garlic with a good-quality chef's knife. Don't try to chop with a paring knife; it's an awkward tool for the task. Slice the clove lengthwise as thin as you can and then give it a quarter turn and slice it thin again. Chop this pile of tiny garlic cubes as fine as possible. The garlic will tend to fan out as you chop; just use your knife to scrape it back into a pile and continue chopping.
>
> Occasionally, garlic will germinate and produce green sprouts, which taste bitter if eaten raw. If the cloves are still firm, however, the garlic is fine. To get rid of the sprout, just cut the clove in half through the center of the sprout and peel each sprout-half away from the clove.

Pressing Garlic

- Some cooks think that garlic squeezed through a press gives it an unpalatably strong taste. Try it, taste it, and decide for yourself.

- Some feel that while a press saves you peeling time (put the clove in the press and squeeze—the garlic flesh is forced out of the press while the skin stays in), it takes more time to thoroughly clean the press than it's worth. Again, try it and decide for yourself.

- Clean a press as soon as you're finished using it, before the leftover garlic dries and clogs the holes, or let it soak in a glass of hot water until you're ready to clean it. It's important to make sure it gets very clean, because if residual oil from the garlic hangs on, the oil gets rancid quickly and will be passed on to the next clove of garlic you press.

  If you have a stainless-steel or a plastic press (even if it's a *self-cleaning* unit) that's dishwasher-safe, open the press and spread it out on the bottom rack or across the silverware container of the dishwasher and let it run through a normal cycle.

Cooking Garlic

- Crushed, chopped, diced, minced, or pressed garlic produces a more pungent, assertive taste than whole or sliced cloves.

- The longer garlic cooks, the milder it tastes. For a stronger flavor, either add it just before the dish is done cooking, or add raw garlic to the completed dish.

- Garlic burns easily when sautéing. Sauté over medium heat, stirring constantly. Don't overbrown it. Overbrowned garlic tastes bitter. When sautéing both garlic and onions, do the onions first. When they're just about done, add the garlic so that it doesn't get overbrowned.

Roasting Garlic

Recipes for roasted garlic are included in the Recipes section. Here are tips to enhance the taste:

- Use a good, fruity olive oil. Extra virgin is fine but not necessary. Just stay away from oils labeled "light."
- The roasting time and temperature most often recommended is: 325–350 degrees for 45 minutes to an hour.
- If you don't have a terra cotta garlic roaster, use an unglazed (thoroughly cleaned) terra cotta flowerpot that has a 6-inch saucer with a high rim. Soak both pieces in clean, warm water for 15 minutes, then put 1 to 4 average heads of garlic in the saucer, prepare them according to your recipe, then cover with the flowerpot.
- If you don't have an appropriate roasting container for garlic, aluminum foil works fine.
- As for the microwave . . . yes, you can roast garlic, but it won't have that real *roasted* flavor. It will taste more like steamed garlic. And it will be off-white instead of an appealing caramel color.
- Yes, garlic can be roasted over the dying embers of a grill. Oil the outside of the bulb and set it down directly on the grill. Keep on it, checking the color and consistency (test-squeeze it every now and then) to know when it's done.

Aioli's Allure

Any book that deals with garlic as food must make mention of *aioli*. It's a rich sauce, typically made of crushed garlic, egg yolks, lemon juice, and olive oil, used especially to garnish fish and vegetables.

Instead of the traditional aioli, here is the Mediterranean style, which seems safer because it does not require *raw* egg yolks: Simply squeeze out the insides of a few roasted garlic cloves and mix the purée into plain mayonnaise (regular or low-fat), blending thoroughly.

Garlic As Garnish

Cut a few peeled garlic cloves into thin slices. Over a medium heat, heat a little olive oil, add the garlic slices, and stir often for about 5 minutes, until the garlic is a dark golden to light brown. Remove the slices with a slotted spoon and use them to garnish an appropriate dish.

Garlic and Salads

- To subtly garlic-flavor salads, rub the inside of the salad serving bowl(s) with the juicy side of a half clove of garlic before adding salad ingredients.
- Season a salad French style with a *chapon*. Rub garlic on a big chunk of stale Italian or French bread and toss it with the salad. Remove the bread (*chapon*) right before you serve the salad.
- Even more subtle is the technique of Queen Victoria's chef, who would chew a clove of garlic and then breathe over the salad immediately before serving.

Garlic Salt

As you can imagine, garlic salt is high in sodium—about 900 milligrams in 1 teaspoon. The minimum average requirement for sodium in adults is 500 mg a day, not to exceed 2400 mg a day. It's wiser to use garlic powder and salt to taste.

Garlic Vinegar (See Preparations chapter.)

Garlic Yields

1 fresh medium garlic clove = 1/2 teaspoon minced
1/8 teaspoon dried minced
1/8 teaspoon garlic powder
Each average size roasted head of garlic = 4 tablespoons garlic purée

Deodorizing
(Breath, Hands, Cutting Board, and Microwave)

Breath: (See GARLIC BREATH in Remedies chapter.)

Hands:

- Take a piece of silverware (stainless steel will do), pretend it's a cake of soap, and wash your hands with it under cold water. The garlic smell will vanish in seconds. (See the Resources chapter for a similar hand-deodorizing product.)

- Rub hands with celery or tomato or lemon or fresh ginger. If that doesn't do it, then follow it up by rubbing salt on your hands. Rinse and wash with soap and warm water. (Also see the Resources chapter for companies that have commercial products that help remove garlic odor from hands.)

Cutting Board:
- Rub it with a wedge of lemon and kosher (coarse) salt.
- Make a paste of baking soda and water and rub the board with it.

Microwave:
- Cook some slices of cucumber for a few minutes.

NUTRITIONAL VALUES

3-1/2 OUNCES RAW GARLIC (33 CLOVES)

Calories	149
Protein	6 g
Carbohydrates	33 g
Sodium	17 mg
Fat	less than 1 g
Saturated Fat	less than 1 g
Cholesterol	0 mg
Vitamin B1/Thiamin	0.2 mg
Vitamin B6	1.2 mg
Vitamin C	31 mg
Calcium	181 mg
Iron	2 mg
Copper	0.3 mg
Manganese	1.7 mg
Phosphorus	153 mg
Potassium	401 mg

Recipes

I consider the smell of garlic—raw, sautéed, roasted,
or stewed—to be always a promise of good food and
at times practically an aphrodisiac.

Barbara Kafka

This is an eclectic collection of recipes—something for everyone who loves garlic. Naturally, you can increase or decrease the amount of garlic in each recipe in keeping with your tolerance, taste buds, and social life.

The recipes, along with any accompanying comments, came to us from many sources: family, friends, restaurants, chefs, cookbook authors, garlic festivals, organizations, associations, companies, food specialty shops, and the Garlic Information Center.

The recipes range from heart-smart to pig heaven; from complex, for those who know their way around a kitchen, to simple, for those who need a map to *find* the kitchen.

The oven settings are always degrees in Farenheit.

Whenever available, nutritional values (calories, protein, fat, carbohydrates, sodium, etc.) have been included.

APPETIZERS

A little garlic, judiciously used, won't seriously affect
your social life, and will tone up more dull dishes
than any commodity discovered to date.

Alexander Wright
How to Live Without a Woman, 1937

GARLIC BASIL CUSTARD

The Stinking Cookbook by Jerry Dal Bozzo
The Stinking Rose: A Garlic Restaurant
San Francisco and Los Angeles

Ingredients for 6 to 7 servings:
3 cups milk
1/2 teaspoon freshly chopped garlic
6 eggs, whole

3 egg yolks
1/2 cup freshly chopped basil
salt and pepper to taste

1. Place milk and garlic in medium saucepan and bring to a boil.
2. Whip the eggs in a nonreactive bowl and while stirring, add scalded milk.
3. Process the basil and egg mixture in a food processor. Add salt and pepper to taste.
4. Strain through a fine-mesh strainer and fill six 8-ounce ovenproof soufflé cups.
5. Place cups in a baking pan half-filled with hot water.
6. Bake at 325 degrees for 1 hour or until a toothpick comes out clean when inserted into center of custard.
7. Let cool for 10 minutes. Run a paring knife around the edge of the custard, place a plate over the top of the cup, invert and gently shake the custard onto the plate.
8. Serve with marinara sauce.

WHOLE ROASTED GARLIC WITH ASADERO OR BRIE CHEESE AND TOMATILLO-CILANTRO SALSA

Katharine Kagel
Cafe Pasqual's Cookbook
(Chronicle Books, Santa Fe, 1993)

This simple yet sumptuous recipe is a United Nations plate. The whole roasted garlic is a staple Italian dish, the *asadero* is a contemporary melt-away white Mexican cheese, and the salsa is from Old Mexico. Or you can choose to put France on the plate by using Brie in place of the *asadero*.

Thanks go to my brother Peter for this dish. On seven different occasions he sent me the menu from his favorite Italian restaurant in San Francisco with the roasted garlic offering circled. Finally, I developed this appetizer and have been grateful to him ever since!

Set out oyster forks for the guests to use to lift the roasted garlic cloves whole from their skins. The cloves will spread like softened butter on a piece of French bread or warmed flour tortilla. Also, out of respect for Peter's abhorrence of cilantro, please note that Italian flat-leaf parsley may be substituted for the cilantro in the salsa.

Ingredients to serve 4:
4 whole bulbs garlic
1/4 cup olive oil

Ingredients for the tomatillo-cilantro salsa:
1/3 pound tomatillos, husks removed
1/2 small white onion, chopped
1 clove garlic
1 fresh *serrano* chile, stemmed
1/4 cup water
1/2 teaspoon salt
1/2 bunch fresh cilantro (coriander) or flat-leaf parsley, stemmed
6 ounces *asadero* cheese or Brie cheese, cut into 4 equal pieces
1 loaf French bread, sliced, or 12 white-flour or whole-wheat tortillas, warmed

Preheat oven to 375 degrees.
To prepare the garlic bulbs for roasting, remove the excess papery skin but leave the bulbs whole. Cut off the top 1/2 inch of each bulb, exposing the tops of the individual garlic cloves. If some of the clove tops remain uncut, take a little slice off each with a paring knife to expose the inside.
Place the garlic bulbs, cut sides up, in a deep-sided casserole or loaf pan and add water to reach halfway up the sides of the bulbs. Drizzle the olive oil evenly over the tops of the bulbs. Cover tightly with aluminum foil and place in the oven. Bake until the cloves feel soft when pressed, about 1 hour.

Meanwhile, prepare the salsa. Place the tomatillos, onion, garlic, chile, and water in a blender or a food processor fitted with the metal blade. Add the cilantro or parsley and whirl until smooth. Do not add the cilantro or parsley until just before serving or it will lose its flavor and bright-green color. You will have about 3/4 cup salsa.

To serve, preheat a broiler. Place a piece of the cheese on each of 4 flameproof serving plates. Run the plates under the broiler until the cheese just begins to melt, 3 to 5 minutes. Be careful not to allow the cheese to melt into a puddle. Place a garlic bulb next to the cheese and flood the plate with the salsa. Accompany with French bread or tortillas.

GARLIC FRITTERS

Marilou Robinson
Northwest Garlic Festival

Ingredients for 15 to 20 fritters:

3/4 cup flour
1 tablespoon yellow cornmeal
1 tablespoon sugar
2 teaspoons baking powder
2 teaspoons allspice
1 teaspoon salt
3 tablespoons freshly minced parsley
1/2 teaspoon hot sauce or to taste
3/4 cup milk
1/2 cup peeled and finely minced garlic
2 cups finely minced green onion
vegetable oil for frying

In a large bowl, mix flour, cornmeal, sugar, baking powder, allspice, and salt. Stir in parsley, hot sauce, and milk till well blended. Add garlic and onion and mix well.

Pour 1 inch oil into an electric skillet and heat at 360 to 370 degrees. Drop batter by teaspoonfuls into hot oil and

*flatten slightly. Fry till golden brown on the bottom; turn
and fry till second side is golden brown, about 5 minutes
total. Remove to paper towels to drain. Keep warm in a
low oven till all are done.*

    Serve as an appetizer, or as a side dish.

VEGGIE PÂTÉ

Cherie Calbom & Vicki Rae Chelf
Cooking for Life
(Avery Publishing Group, 1993)

A truly delicious vitamin-packed pâté to spread on bread or
crackers.

*Ingredients for 10 to 12 appetizer servings,
or 4 to 6 sandwich servings:*
1 pound potatoes (approximately 3 small)
4 medium carrots
1 bunch (1/4 pound) spinach
3 large leaves kale
1 cup sunflower seeds
1/4 cup whole wheat pastry flour
1/4 cup nutritional yeast
1/4 cup tamari
1/2 teaspoon sage
1/2 teaspoon marjoram
5 cloves garlic, pressed
pinch cayenne pepper
juice extractor (juicing machine)

Preheat the oven to 350 degrees.
    *Cut the potatoes into chunks. Cut the greens off the carrots. Bunch up the spinach and kale leaves, and juice them
with the potato chunks. Combine all of the spinach, kale,
and potato juices and pulps in a large bowl. Separately
juice just enough of the carrots to make 1/2 cup of juice;
add the 1/2 cup of juice and all of the pulp to the bowl.*

In a blender, grind the sunflower seeds to a powder. Add them to the combined juice and pulp in the bowl, along with the pastry flour, nutritional yeast, tamari, sage, marjoram, garlic, and cayenne pepper; mix well.

Transfer the mixture to a well-oiled 8-by-8-inch baking dish. Bake, uncovered, until a toothpick inserted into the center of the mixture comes out clean, about 50 minutes. Let the pâté cool for at least 2 hours before serving it.

To serve the pâté, cut it into squares. Accompany it with whole grain bread or crackers. For a delicious sandwich, spread a generous portion of pâte on one slice of whole grain bread, spread mustard on the other slice of bread, and garnish the sandwich with tomato and lettuce.

(Preparation time: 30 minutes; baking time: 50 minutes; cooling time: 2 hours.)

STUFFED MUSHROOMS WITH GARLIC

Fran Comandini
"Garlicfest"
Fairfield, Connecticut

Ingredients:
1 basket medium-sized mushrooms
6 cloves garlic, mashed
1 tablespoon basil
1/2 cup oil
3 cups grated cheese of your choice (e.g., Swiss, Jarlsberg, Cheddar)
1 tablespoon dried parsley
1/2 teaspoon black pepper
1/8 cup water

Wash mushrooms, remove stems and peel off outer skin. Mix all other ingredients together (except water) and stuff each mushroom with 1 teaspoon of mixture and pat down. Add water to pan, then line up stuffed mushrooms in pan. Cover with foil and bake at 350 degrees for 35 to 40 minutes.

BEANS AND GRAINS

*Its heat is very vehement; and all vehement hot things
send up but ill-savored vapors to the brain . . . it
will . . . send up strong fancies, and as many strange
visions to the head; therefore, let it be taken inwardly
with great moderation.*

Nicholas Culpeper

APPALOOSA BEAN AND FENNEL SALAD

Ted Matern
Dean & Deluca
New York, New York

Ingredients:

1 package (1 pound) Dean & Deluca appaloosa beans or can-
nellini beans or great northern beans
1 fennel bulb
1 whole garlic bulb
1/4 cup Dean & Deluca kalamata vinegar or red wine vinegar
1/3 cup olive oil
1/4 cup finely minced parsley
1 teaspoon salt
freshly ground black pepper to taste

*Place the beans in a pot, cover with cold water, and bring
to a boil. Drain and add fresh water. Bring to a boil,
reduce heat, and simmer until tender (40 to 50 minutes).
Remove from heat and let beans cool in water rather than
air to prevent skins from splitting open.*

*Bring water to a boil in a small saucepan, add the whole
garlic bulb. Allow garlic to simmer for 2 minutes. Remove
the garlic bulb, peel all the cloves, and put into a food
processor. Add the vinegar, and turn on the processor. Add
the oil slowly and blend all the ingredients.*

Cut the fennel bulb in half from top to bottom. Remove any brown edges, and slice into thin strips. Drain the beans, and put into a large mixing bowl, along with the sliced fennel. Add the garlic, oil, and vinegar mixture. Add the chopped parsley, salt, and pepper, and mix well. Allow to set for at least 2 hours, or refrigerate overnight, then serve at room temperature on a bed of romaine or red leaf lettuce.

BROWN RICE BLACK BEAN BURRITO

USA Rice Council

Ingredients for 6 servings:
1 tablespoon vegetable oil
1 medium onion, chopped
2 cloves garlic, minced
1-1/2 teaspoons chili power
1/2 teaspoon cumin
3 cups cooked brown rice
1 can (15–16 ounces) black beans, drained and rinsed
1 can (11 ounces) corn, drained
6 (8-inch) flour tortillas
3/4 cup (6 ounces) shredded reduced-fat cheddar cheese
2 green onions, thinly sliced
1/4 cup plain low-fat yogurt
1/4 cup prepared salsa

Heat oil in large skillet over medium-high heat until hot. Add onion, garlic, chili powder, and cumin. Sauté 3 to 5 minutes until onion is tender. Add rice, beans, and corn; cook, stirring 2 to 3 minutes until mixture is thoroughly heated. Remove from heat. Spoon 1/2 cup rice mixture down center of each tortilla. Top each with 2 tablespoons cheese, 1 tablespoon green onion, and 1 tablespoon yogurt; roll up, top with 1 tablespoon salsa.

GARLIC RICE SALAD

Jo Ann F. Doyer
Northwest Garlic Festival

Ingredients:
1/3 cup wild rice
1-3/4 cups water
10 cloves fresh, peeled, and chopped garlic
1/8 teaspoon salt
1/2 cup long-grain rice
2 tablespoons salad oil
2 tablespoons rice vinegar or white vinegar
2 teaspoons soy sauce
2 teaspoons honey
1/4 teaspoon ground ginger
1/4 cup slivered almonds, toasted
1 package (6 ounces) frozen pea pods

Rinse wild rice under cold water about 1 minute. In a small saucepan, bring the wild rice, water, garlic, and salt to boiling. Reduce heat. Cover and simmer 30 minutes. Stir in the long-grain rice; return to boiling. Reduce heat. Cover and simmer 15 to 20 minutes more or till water is absorbed and rice is done. Remove from heat. Let it stand, covered, for 10 minutes.

Dressing: In a small screwtop jar, combine oil, vinegar, soy sauce, honey, and ginger. Cover and shake well.

Transfer rice to a bowl. Pour dressing over rice mixture. Toss to coat. Cover and chill at least 3 hours.

At serving time, place pea pods in a colander; rinse under warm water to thaw. Add pea pods and toasted almonds to salad; toss to coat.

SOUTHWEST VEGETABLE PAELLA

(An American Southwest interpretation
of this Spanish favorite)

USA Rice Council

Ingredients for 6 servings:

1 tablespoon vegetable oil

1 medium onion, cut into 1/2-inch pieces

1 medium-sized green bell pepper, cut into 1/2-inch pieces

2 cloves garlic, minced

1 cup uncooked rice (recipe based on regular-milled long-grain white rice)

1 can (14-1/2 ounces) chicken broth

1 can (10 ounces) diced tomatoes and green chilies (1 8-ounce jar picante sauce may be substituted)

1/4 teaspoon turmeric

1 can (15–16 ounces) black beans, drained and rinsed

1 can (11 ounces) corn, drained

Heat oil in large skillet over medium-high heat until hot. Add onion, bell pepper, and garlic; cook 3 to 5 minutes or until onion is tender. Add rice, broth, tomatoes and green chilies, and turmeric. Bring to a boil; reduce heat; cover and simmer 15 minutes. Stir in beans and corn; cook 2 to 3 minutes or until thoroughly heated.

NUTRIENTS PER SERVING

Calories 256
Protein. . . . . 9 g
Fat . . . . 4 g
Cholesterol. . . . . 0 mg
Dietary fiber. . . . . . . 4 g
Carbohydrates . . . . . 48 g
Sodium . . . . 389 mg

WALNUT LEMON COUSCOUS

Walnut Marketing Board

Ingredients for 3 cups/4 servings:
2 tablespoons olive oil
1 cup walnut pieces
2 large cloves garlic, pressed
2/3 cup chicken bouillon or broth
1/4 cup fresh lemon juice
1/2 cup sliced green onions
1/2 cup sliced, pitted ripe olives
4 thin lemon slices, quartered
3/4 cup instant couscous
salt and pepper to taste

In an 8- to 10-inch skillet, heat oil over medium heat. Add walnuts and garlic; toss 2 minutes. Add bouillon, lemon juice, onions, olives, and lemon pieces. Bring to boiling. Stir in couscous. Remove from heat; cover and set aside for 5 minutes. Toss with fork; season with salt and pepper.
Serve immediately with baked or broiled chicken.

PEANUT-BARLEY STUFFING

Oklahoma Peanut Commission

Peanuts and barley, when paired together in adequate amounts, form a complete protein, which means that they provide the 8 essential amino acids that our body does not manufacture and must get from the foods we eat.

Ingredients for about 3 cups:
1-1/2 cups quick-cooking pearled barley
water for cooking barley
1-1/2 teaspoons beef-flavored instant bouillon
1 tablespoon vegetable oil
1 cup chopped onion
1 clove garlic, crushed

1 can (4 ounces) mushroom stems and pieces, chopped
1 cup chopped peanuts
1/4 cup chopped parsley
1 tablespoon fresh lemon juice
1/2 teaspoon thyme leaves
dash of cayenne pepper

Cook barley according to package directions, adding beef bouillon to water. Cook until all water is absorbed. In a saucepan, sauté onion and garlic in oil until tender; add mushrooms and continue cooking several minutes. Stir into cooked barley along with peanuts, parsley, lemon juice, thyme, and pepper.

It's a super stuffing for vegetables—peppers, tomatoes, cabbage, or eggplant—and for fish, poultry, and meat. Will stuff 6 to 8 thick pork chops with about 1/2 cup stuffing per chop. It's also a tasty side dish.

BEEF, PORK, AND LAMB

Garlic is the ketchup of intellectuals.

Unknown

GARLIC-MUSHROOM STUFFED SIRLOIN

Texas Beef Organization

Ingredients for 8 to 10 servings:
3 pounds beef top sirloin steak, cut 2 inches thick
1 tablespoon olive oil
1 cup finely chopped fresh mushrooms (about 3 ounces)
1/4 cup garlic cloves, finely chopped
1/2 cup thinly sliced green onions
1 tablespoon dry red wine
1/4 teaspoon each: salt, dried thyme leaves, pepper

Heat oil in nonstick skillet over medium heat. Add mushrooms, garlic, and green onions; cook 4 minutes or until tender, stirring occasionally. Add wine and cook until evaporated. Stir in salt, thyme, and pepper. Remove from heat; cool.

Make a horizontal cut through center of steak, approximately 1/2 inch from each side, parallel to surface of steak, to form a pocket. Cut to, but not through, opposite side. Spoon stuffing into pocket, spreading evenly. Close opening with toothpicks. Roast sirloin in a 350-degree oven on a rack in a shallow roasting pan for 1 hour, or 20 minutes per pound.

Remove steak from oven and let stand 10 to 15 minutes covered with foil tent. Remove toothpicks and carve into 1/2-inch-thick slices.

Serving suggestion: Mashed potatoes and glazed carrots.

STEAK WITH PARMESAN-GRILLED VEGETABLES

National Cattlemen's Beef Association

Ingredients for 4 servings:

2 well-trimmed beef T-bone or porterhouse steaks, cut 1-inch thick (approximately 2 pounds)

1/4 cup grated Parmesan cheese

2 tablespoons olive oil

2 tablespoons red wine vinegar

2 medium red or yellow bell peppers, each cut lengthwise into quarters

1 large red onion, cut crosswise into 1/2-inch slices

salt to taste

Seasoning:

1 tablespoon crushed garlic

2 teaspoons dried basil leaves

1 teaspoon pepper

1. In small bowl, combine seasoning ingredients; mix well. Remove 4 teaspoons seasoning; press into both sides of beef steaks.

2. Add cheese, oil, and vinegar to remaining seasoning, mixing well; set aside.
3. Place steaks in center of grill over medium ash-covered coals; arrange vegetables around steaks. Grill steaks uncovered 14 to 16 minutes and vegetables 15 to 20 minutes or until tender, turning both once. Brush vegetables with reserved cheese mixture during last 10 minutes of grilling.
4. Season steaks with salt, as desired. Trim fat from steaks; remove bones. Carve steaks crosswise into thick slices; serve with vegetables.

(Total preparation and cooking time: 30 minutes. Calories per serving: 320; fat grams per serving: 18)

ELEPHANT STEAKS

Frieda's, Inc.

Ingredients for 2 servings:
2 beef steaks
1 tablespoon cooking oil
3 cloves elephant garlic, peeled and thinly sliced (true garlic cloves may be substituted)
1/4 cup beef broth
1/3 cup dry red wine
1 tablespoon minced parsley
1 teaspoon Worcestershire sauce
1/2 teaspoon Dijon mustard
1/4 teaspoon pepper
2 slices crusty French bread, toasted

Broil steaks 4 inches from heat source, turning once, till cooked to desired doneness (about 10 minutes total for medium-rare for 1-inch-thick steaks).
Meanwhile, prepare sauce: in a skillet heat oil; sauté elephant garlic for 3 minutes or till almost tender. Stir in beef broth, wine, parsley, Worcestershire sauce, Dijon mustard, and pepper. Cook and stir; bring to boiling. Boil 1 minute. Place steaks on toast; spoon sauce over.

FIESTA MEAT BALLS PIQUANTE

USA Rice Council

Ingredients for 3 dozen meat balls:
1 pound lean ground beef
1 medium onion, minced and divided
3 cloves garlic, minced and divided
2 tablespoons chopped cilantro, divided
1 tablespoon paprika
1 teaspoon salt
1/2 teaspoon ground black pepper
2 eggs, slightly beaten
3/4 cup uncooked rice
vegetable cooking spray
2 cans (15 ounces each) tomato sauce
1 cup beef broth
2 chilpotle peppers, pickled
1 tablespoon chili powder

Combine beef, 2 tablespoons onion, 1 clove garlic, 1 tablespoon cilantro, paprika, salt, pepper, eggs, and rice. Mix well and shape into 1-1/2-inch meatballs. Place in large baking dish coated with cooking spray. Combine tomato sauce, broth, remaining onion, peppers, chili powder, and remaining garlic in blender jar. Cover and process until smooth. Place tomato sauce in large skillet; cook over medium-high heat, stirring constantly 3 to 5 minutes. Pour sauce over meat balls and bake covered at 350 degrees for 1 hour or until rice is tender. Sprinkle with remaining cilantro. Serve hot.

BEEF AND VEGETABLE FRIED RICE

National Cattlemen's Beef Association

Ingredients for 4 (1-1/2) cup servings:
1 pound lean ground beef
2 cloves garlic, crushed
1 teaspoon grated fresh ginger or 1/4 teaspoon ground ginger

2 tablespoons water

1 red bell pepper, cut into 1/2-inch pieces

1 package (6 ounces) frozen pea pods

3 cups cold cooked rice

3 tablespoons soy sauce

2 teaspoons dark sesame oil

1/4 cup green onions, thinly sliced

1. In large nonstick skillet, brown ground beef, garlic, and ginger over medium heat 8 to 10 minutes or until beef is no longer pink, breaking it up into 3/4-inch crumbles. Remove with slotted spoon; pour off drippings.
2. In same skillet, heat water over medium-high heat until hot. Add bell pepper and pea pods; cook 3 minutes or until bell pepper is crisp-tender, stirring occasionally. Add rice, soy sauce, and seasame oil; mix well. Return beef to skillet; heat through, about 5 minutes. Stir in green onions before serving.

NUTRIENTS PER SERVING

Calories...................... 423
Protein .... 28 g
Fat............................. 12 g
Cholesterol .... 70 mg
Carbohydrates .... 50 g
Iron .... 5.3 mg
Sodium...................... 843 mg

CHALUPA

California Dry Bean Advisory Board

Ingredients:

1 pound dry pink beans

3 pounds pork roast

1/2 cup chopped onion

2 cloves garlic, minced

1 tablespoon salt

2 tablespoons chili powder
1 tablespoon cumin
1 teaspoon oregano
1 can (4 ounces) chopped green chilies
corn chips
toppings (suggestions below)

*Sort and rinse beans. Put all ingredients, except corn
chips, in Dutch oven, an electric crockery cooker, or heavy
kettle. Add 7 cups water. Cover and simmer about 5 hours,
or until roast falls apart and beans are done. Uncover and
cook about 1/2 hour to desired thickness.*

*Serve with corn chips and prepare condiments (chopped
tomato, avocado, onion, shredded lettuce, grated cheddar
cheese, taco sauce, or other hot sauce) as topping(s).*

GARLIC-RUBBED LAMB LOIN

Luke David Schultheis
Director of Food and Beverage
The Mayflower Hotel
New York, New York

Ingredients:
1 8-ounce loin of lamb, cleaned
3 ounces bread crumbs
1 ounce pecorino Romano cheese
1/2 ounce spicy horseradish
1/2 tablespoon pommery mustard
1 roasted garlic bulb (see Index for Roasted Garlic recipe)
2 cloves raw garlic, halved
juice of 2 lemons

*Mix roast garlic, mustard, horseradish, lemon, cheese, and
breadcrumbs. Slice small holes in lamb and fully insert
half cloves of garlic. Rub exterior of lamb with above mixture, and roast at 400 degrees until it's as well done as you
want it to be. Slice and fan along plate.*

*Serve with ratatouille and sautéed spinach with
browned garlic.*

BREADS, MUFFINS, CLOUDS, AND CROUTONS

It is not really an exaggeration to say that peace and happiness begin, geographically, where garlic is used in cooking.

X. Marcel Boulestin

GARLIC TOAST

Vicki Rae Chelf
Cooking With the Right Side of the Brain
(Avery Publishing Group, 1991)

Ingredients for 10 to 12 slices:
1/4 cup olive oil
6 to 8 cloves garlic, pressed
2 teaspoons tamari
10 to 12 slices whole grain bread
optional: 1 tablespoon finely minced parsley

1. In a small bowl, mix together the oil, garlic, tamari, and parsley.
2. Spread the mixture over sliced whole grain bread. Toast for a minute or two under the broiler or in a toaster oven.
3. Serve hot with soup, vegetable-based main dishes, or salad.

    You may store this garlic mixture in a small covered container in the refrigerator and use it as needed, but don't keep it longer than 2 weeks.
(*Preparation time:* 10 minutes.)

GARLIC BRUSCHETTA

Luke David Schultheis
Director of Food and Beverage
The Mayflower Hotel, New York, New York

Ingredients:
1 thick slice of sourdough bread
1 clove garlic, peeled

1 large garlic bulb, unpeeled
1 ripe plum tomato
2 tablespoons balsamic vinegar
2 fresh leaves of opal or green basil
kosher (coarse) salt and pepper

Cut off top of unpeeled garlic bulb and brush with extra virgin olive oil and kosher salt. Wrap in foil and roast slowly at 300 degrees for 45 minutes to an hour.

Cut up tomato into small pieces, sprinkle pepper on the pieces and marinate with basil in vinegar. As garlic bulb softens, rub bread with the clove of raw garlic, brush with oil, and grill until hot.

To serve: Cut bread in two, diagonally, resting one corner on the other half slice. Cascade the tomato salad over the middle onto the plate, and place the roasted bulb in the rear of the bread. Press on the cloves of the bulb to extract the sweet, roasted garlic, and eat with the salad and bread.

BRUSCHETTA WITH TOMATOES, BLUE CHEESE, AND PECANS

Florida Tomato Committee

Bruschetta is a type of Italian garlic bread, the perfect foundation for all sorts of wonderful toppings. This version uses a blend of cheeses mixed with pecans, topped with fresh (Florida) tomatoes, and basil. Serve as an appetizer, with soup, stew, or pasta dishes. Use the best rustic country bread you can find.

Ingredients for 4 servings:
2 ounces cream cheese, softened
1/2 cup crumbled blue cheese
2 tablespoons coarsely chopped pecans
4 slices crusty, firm-textured bread, cut about 3/4-inch thick
2 cloves garlic, peeled and halved
2 large (Florida) tomatoes, sliced about 1/8-inch thick
freshly ground pepper to taste
chopped fresh basil or dried basil for garnish

1. In a small bowl, mash the cheeses together with a fork, leaving the mixture somewhat chunky. Mix in the pecans.
2. Preheat the broiler. Arrange the bread on a small baking sheet and broil the slices for about a minute on each side—just until golden. Watch it carefully so it doesn't burn.
3. Rub one side of each piece of bread with garlic.
4. Spread some of the cheese mixture over each slice and arrange 2 or 3 overlapping tomato slices on top. Pepper the tomatoes lightly, then garnish with basil and serve.

EASY ELEPHANT GARLIC FOCCACIA BREAD

Frieda's, Inc.

This easy garlic bread goes well with a salad or soup, or served as an appetizer with before-dinner libations.

Ingredients for 16 pieces:
1 can (8 ounces) refrigerated pizza dough
3 tablespoons light olive oil or vegetable oil
2 cloves elephant garlic, peeled and sliced into very thin julienne sticks (true garlic cloves may be substituted)
2 tablespoons fresh chives, chopped
2 tablespoons fresh basil, chopped
1 tablespoon fresh sage, chopped

Press pizza dough into a greased 13-by-9-by-2-inch baking dish. In skillet heat 2 tablespoons oil; sauté garlic for 4 minutes over low heat, stirring frequently (do not allow garlic to burn). Stir in chives, basil, and sage. Brush bread dough with remaining 1 tablespoon oil. Spread garlic mixture generously over bread dough. Bake in preheated 425-degree oven for 8 to 10 minutes, or until golden brown at edges. Cut into 16 squares and serve hot.

GARLIC AND HERB BAGEL CHIPS

Sandra Woodruff, R.D.
Fat-Free Holiday Recipes
(Avery Publishing Group, 1995)

Ingredients for 8 servings:
4 whole wheat or oat bran bagels
2 teaspoons crushed fresh garlic
2 teaspoons dried Italian seasoning
2 tablespoons grated nonfat or reduced-fat Parmesan cheese
olive oil cooking spray

1. Slice the bagels diagonally into 1/4-inch-thick slices. Coat the inside of a large bowl with the garlic, and sprinkle the Italian seasoning over the garlic coating. Place the bagel chips in the bowl, and toss gently until the chips are coated with the garlic and herbs. Sprinkle the cheese over the chips, and again toss gently to coat.
2. Coat a baking sheet with olive oil cooking spray. Arrange the chips on the sheet in a single layer, and spray the tops of the chips very lightly with the cooking spray. Bake at 350 degrees for 6 minutes. Turn the chips over and bake for an additional 5 to 8 minutes, or until lightly browned and crisp. Cool to room temperature.
3. Serve the chips with spreads or dips. (See the SPREADS, SAUCES, DIPS, etc. section.)

NUTRIENTS PER SERVING

Calories...................... 95
Protein .... 3.8 g
Fat............................. 0.4 g
Cholesterol .... 0 mg
Fiber .... 1.6 g
Sodium...................... 165 mg

MAMA MIA MUFFINS

Gloria Ambrosia
Gloria's Glorious Muffins
(Avery Publishing Group, 1993)

Basically, this is garlic bread in a muffin, and it goes with just about everything. Enjoy it as you would garlic bread.

For 12 muffins:

Dry Ingredients:
3 cups whole wheat pastry flour
1/2 cup unbleached white flour
1 tablespoon baking powder
1/2 teaspoon sea salt
1/2 teaspoon paprika

Wet Ingredients:
2 cups vegetable broth
1/2 cup olive oil
1 egg

Goodies:
5 cloves minced garlic
1 tablespoon dried basil
1 teaspoon dried oregano
3/4 cup grated Parmesan cheese

Topping:
sprinkling of paprika and grated Parmesan cheese

1. Preheat oven to 400 degrees.
2. Measure and sift the dry ingredients together in a large bowl. Sift a second time. Set aside.
3. Whisk the wet ingredients in a medium bowl or blend them in your food processor using the purée blade.
4. Add the goodies to the wet ingredients and stir to combine.

5. Pour the wet ingredients into the dry ingredients. Stir just until mixed. *Do not overstir.*

6. Spoon the batter into greased or papered baking tins. Fill each cup nearly to the top.

7. Top each muffin with a sprinkling of paprika and grated Parmesan cheese.

8. Bake for 15 to 20 minutes.

9. Cool in the baking tins for at least 10 minutes.

GOLDEN GARLIC CLOUDS

The Garlic Lovers Cookbook, Vols. I & II
The Gilroy Garlic Festival Association, Inc.

Fascinating Yorkshire Pudding Popovers with pizazz! A quick, glorious accompaniment to roasts, steaks, and stews. Makes even the simplest of meat dishes seem extra special.

Jeanne Howard was second runner-up with this recipe in the 1980 Gilroy Garlic Festival recipe contest.

Ingredients for 8 large clouds:
shortening, bacon grease, or fat drippings from a roast
2 eggs
1/2 cup whole milk
6 or more cloves of fresh garlic or 1 teaspoon garlic powder
1 teaspoon dried Bouquet Garni, well crushed
1/2 cup all-purpose flour, unsifted
1/2 teaspoon salt
1/8 teaspoon baking powder

Preheat oven to 450 degrees. Be sure all ingredients are room temperature. Prepare large muffin pan (preferably cast iron) by greasing generously with shortening. Heat in oven until fat spits. Beat eggs well. Add milk and mix together either by electric mixer or by hand. If using fresh garlic, peel and put through garlic press and add the resulting juice. If using garlic powder, sift with dry ingredients. Sift dry ingredients together, add to milk mixture, and beat until thoroughly blended. Remove muffin pan from oven and quickly pour batter in each muffin pan section to about 1/2 full. Immediately return to oven and bake 20 minutes without opening oven.

To make 16 large clouds, double all ingredients except use only 3 eggs (not 4).

The secret in the preparation is the preheating of the pans. The secret in the eating is the delicious surprise of the garlic and herbs.

ITALIAN WALNUT CROUTONS

Walnut Marketing Board

Ingredients for 8 (1 cup) servings:

1 loaf (8 ounces) baguette-type French bread

1 cup (4 ounces) California walnuts, in large pieces and
   halves

1 egg white

2 tablespoons chopped fresh rosemary or 1 tablespoon dried
   rosemary

3 large cloves garlic, minced

1 tablespoon Worcestershire sauce

2 teaspoons walnut oil or olive oil

1/2 teaspoon salt

1/4 teaspoon cayenne pepper

Preheat oven to 325 degrees. Cut the loaf of bread in half lengthwise, then cut crosswise into thin slices about 1/3-inch thick. Transfer to a large bowl, add the walnuts, and toss to combine. Set aside.

In a small bowl, place the egg whites, rosemary, garlic, Worcestershire, oil, salt, and cayenne pepper. Pour over the bread-and-walnut mixture and toss continuously and vigorously for about 2 minutes, to distribute the seasonings evenly. Transfer the mixture to a large baking pan or roasting pan. Bake for about 30 to 40 minutes, stirring every 10 to 15 minutes, until the pieces of bread are crisp and golden brown and the mixture smells toasted. Remove from the oven and cool completely. Store in an airtight container.

NUTRIENTS PER SERVING

Calories...................... 190
Protein .... 7 g
Total Fat.................... 11 g
Saturated Fat............. 1 g
Calories from Fat....... 100
Cholesterol .... 0 mg
Carbohydrates .... 18 g
Dietary Fiber .... 1 g
Sodium...................... 330 mg

CHICKEN

There are certain dishes in which garlic is the reason for being, and omission would be devastating.

Craig Claiborne

CHIPP CHICKEN

Chipp Prosnit

Ingredients:
(Amounts depend on the number of servings desired.) chicken parts (breasts or thighs), with or without skin; crushed fresh garlic cloves to taste; canned peeled tomatoes, crushed or whole; wheat-free tamari or soy sauce or teriyaki

Preheat oven at 350 to 375 degrees.
In a baking dish, add enough tomatoes to cover the bottom of pan, then spread chicken on top of tomatoes. Rub tomatoes over all exposed chicken sides. Add 1 teaspoon of tamari on each piece of chicken. Smother top of chicken with crushed garlic.

Place in oven. Baste every 10 minutes during 40-minute baking time, or until fork goes through chicken easily.

Then baste one more time and broil chicken for about 3 minutes to turn garlic golden.

GARLIC & THYME CHICKEN OVER GARLIC WILTED SPINACH

Michel Nischan, Chef de Cuisine
Tribeca Grill, Myriad Restaurant Group
New York, New York

Ingredients:

2 breasts of chicken, skin on and first wing joint attached

2 cloves raw garlic, peeled and sliced very thin

1 tablespoon freshly-picked thyme leaves

2 tablespoons extra virgin olive oil

1/4 cup peeled garlic cloves

4 packed cups fresh spinach leaves, well cleaned with ribs removed

salt & pepper to taste

freshly squeezed lemon juice to taste

Carefully insert your finger between the skin and the meat of the chicken breast. See to it that you do not cause the skin to become detached from the breast.

Insert the raw garlic slices between the skin and the flesh, being careful not to overlap. Be sure that the garlic is completely under the skin. This will keep the garlic from burning when you sear the chicken.

Brush the skin of the breast lightly with some of the olive oil. Season with salt, pepper, and half of the thyme leaves.

Heat a medium-sized skillet over a medium flame until very hot. Place the breasts in the skillet, skin-side down, and sauté until the skin begins to crisp. Place the skillet in a 450-degree oven (do not turn the breasts over). Roast for about 5 minutes and then turn the breasts over. Allow to cook an additional 3 to 5 minutes or until the chicken is just done.

Heat the whole garlic cloves with the remaining olive oil in a small-to-medium sauté pan over a medium flame, stirring occasionally, until the garlic becomes golden brown. Turn the heat to high and add the spinach, 1/4 cup at a time, stirring constantly until it wilts. Wait for each 1/4 cup to wilt before adding the other. Season with salt, pepper, and fresh lemon juice.

Push the fully wilted spinach to one side of the pan and allow the juices to run to the opposite side. Reserve the juice.

To serve, place the spinach equally in the center of two plates. Set one chicken breast atop each mound of spinach.

Spoon the juice over all. Sprinkle with remaining thyme leaves.

Serve with sliced, ice-cold vine-ripe tomatoes.

GLAZED XIAN CHICKEN

Martin Yan
Martin Yan's Culinary Journey Through China
(KQED Books) Copyright Yan Can Cook, Inc. 1995

Ingredients for 4 servings:
3/4 pound boneless, skinless chicken
2 tablespoons oyster-flavored sauce

Ingredients for sauce:
1/3 cup chicken broth
3 tablespoons rice wine or dry sherry
2 tablespoons regular soy sauce
2 tablespoons dark soy sauce
1 tablespoon rice vinegar
1-1/2 tablespoons sugar
1 teaspoon chili garlic sauce

2 tablespoons cooking oil
6 small dried red chiles
1 tablespoon minced garlic

2 ribs celery, thinly sliced diagonally
1 small zucchini, thinly sliced diagonally
1 small onion, thinly sliced
optional: 2 teaspoons cornstarch dissolved in 1 tablespoon
   water
1/3 cup toasted walnut halves

1. Cut chicken into 3/4-inch pieces. Place in a bowl and add
   oyster-flavored sauce; stir to coat. Let stand for 10 minutes. Combine sauce ingredients in a bowl; set aside.
2. Place a wok over high heat until hot. Add oil, swirling to
   coat sides. Add chiles and garlic; cook, stirring, until fragrant, about 10 seconds. Add chicken and stir-fry for 1
   minute. Add celery, zucchini, and onion; stir-fry for 30
   seconds. Add sauce and bring to a boil. Reduce heat to low,
   cover, and simmer for 3 minutes. If desired, add cornstarch solution and cook, stirring, until sauce boils and
   thickens. Add walnuts and toss to coat.

BLACK BEAN CHICKEN SALAD
WITH ROASTED GARLIC DRESSING

Frieda's, Inc.

Ingredients for 3 main-dish salads:
2 cloves elephant garlic (or true garlic), peeled
1 teaspoon olive or vegetable oil
1 package (11 ounces) black beans or black-eyed peas,
   cooked according to package directions, and drained
1/2 of a 3-ounce package dried tomatoes, reconstituted
   according to package directions, drained and slivered
1 cup julienne-sliced cooked chicken or turkey
2/3 cup chopped green or yellow bell pepper
1/2 cup diced yellow crookneck squash
1/4 cup white vinegar
1 tablespoon water
2 teaspoons fresh sage, chopped, or 1/2 teaspoon crushed,
   dried sage

2 teaspoons fresh thyme, chopped, or 1/2 teaspoon crushed,
   dried thyme
1/4 teaspoon pepper
lettuce leaves

*Place elephant garlic cloves in a small shallow dish with
oil. Bake covered, in a 325-degree oven for 45 minutes to 1
hour, or till garlic can be easily pierced. Uncover garlic;
cool while preparing salad.*

*In a large bowl combine black beans or black-eyed peas,
dried tomatoes, chicken or turkey, bell pepper, and squash.*

*For dressing, place garlic cloves and oil in a food
processor or blender with vinegar, water, herbs, and pepper. Cover and process until smooth. Drizzle over salad
and toss well. Chill at least 30 minutes to blend flavors.
Spoon salad onto lettuce-lined platter.*

There is no such thing as too much garlic.

Barbara Batcheller

40 CLOVE GARLIC CHICKEN

Authors' Note: As soon as we started working on this book,
we got word out that we wanted "garlic" recipes. And "garlic"
recipes we got. The first one we received was from George
Hartman, for 40 Clove Garlic Chicken. The second one was
from Susan Scheingarten Ruttner, for 40 Clove Garlic
Chicken. And they kept coming, from Eileen Nock, from
Buddy Radisch, from Clipper Mill, from Robert Pardi. . . . Now
that we're up to 260 Clove Garlic Chicken, we're taking a little something from each and giving you what we hope will be
a simple and delicious dish, with thanks to Richard Olney
(who believed it to be an antidote for the "mental antigarlic
quirk"), Paula Peck, and James Beard, all of whom, we were
told, popularized it in their cookbooks in the late 1960s.

Ingredients:

8 pieces of chicken, skinned
2 tablespoons extra virgin olive oil
1 cup onion, minced
2 cups celery, diced
2 tablespoons fresh parsley, minced
1 teaspoon dried tarragon
1/2 cup dry white vermouth
1/2 teaspoon salt
1/4 teaspoon ground pepper
1/2 teaspoon nutmeg
40 cloves garlic, separated but not peeled (about 3 bulbs)

1. Brush chicken pieces on all sides with oil.
2. In a Dutch oven or large casserole dish, combine the onion, celery, parsley, and tarragon. Arrange the chicken pieces on top and pour the vermouth over the chicken. Sprinkle the chicken with salt, pepper, and nutmeg. Distribute the unpeeled garlic cloves throughout the casserole, tucking them under and around the chicken. Tightly cover top of pan or dish with foil.
3. Bake the chicken in a preheated oven at 325 degrees for 1-1/2 hours. No peeking! No kidding!
4. Serve the chicken over rice, barley, or millet, with the garlic. Advise the diners to squeeze the flesh from its papery coat. The garlic is especially tasty when eaten on toast or French bread.

40 CLOVE CHICKEN ARLECCHINO

Lester Mestas
Granito Piedre Grille
Rocklin, California

We couldn't resist including this version of the famous "40 clove" recipe, especially since it's the most popular dish at Lester Mestas' *garlic* restaurant.

Ingredients for 2 servings:
1/3 cup extra virgin olive oil
1 tablespoon butter
3-1/2-pound chicken
3/4 cup flour
1 roasted and peeled red pepper
2 green onions
4 slices mozzarella cheese
2 thin slices prosciutto di parma
40 cloves roasted garlic (see Index for Roasted Garlic
   recipes)
2 teaspoons Dijon mustard
1 cup Marsala wine (Florio brand preferred)
1 cup chicken stock
salt and pepper to taste
4 tablespoons fresh rosemary

1. Remove breasts from chicken, leaving first joint attached, creating the *airline breast*. Remove skin at an angle, and cut breasts open so they unfold.
2. Layer prosciutto, mozzarella, 1/2 of the roasted red pepper, and 1 green onion in each opened breast.
3. Roll breasts so that you have carefully enclosed the stuffing. With string, tie each breast in 2 places, and trim excess green onion.
4. Heat butter and olive oil in a deep heavy skillet.
5. Season breasts with salt, pepper, and rosemary. Toss in flour.
6. When the pan is hot, but not smoking, add the stuffed breasts.
7. Sear breasts on connected side until golden brown, then turn over and place in 450-degree oven for 10 minutes.
8. Remove from oven, drain oil, add Dijon mustard, butter, wine, chicken stock, squeezed-out pulp of the 40 roasted garlic cloves, cover, and simmer for 5 minutes.

9. Remove breasts, cut and remove strings. Turn heat to high and reduce liquid to a creamy consistency.
10. At an angle, cut breasts into 3 pieces, allowing the melted cheese to ooze out. Adjust seasoning and top breasts with 40 clove sauce.

THAI ME UP, THAI ME DOWN

Warren Klein
The Garlic Cafe
Las Vegas, Nevada

Ingredients for 1 serving:
8 ounces diced chicken breast
1 ounce peanut oil
4 diced Thai chilis
3 cloves garlic (or more to taste)
2 ounces sherry
2 ounces diced red bell pepper
2 ounces diced yellow onion
1/2 teaspoon chopped fresh mint
1/2 teaspoon chopped fresh ginger
2 ounces chicken stock
2 ounces black bean garlic sauce (available at Asian markets and at some supermarkets)

1. Place oil, garlic, and chilies in pan over high heat.
2. Sauté until garlic begins to brown.
3. Add chicken, and sauté until all chicken turns white.
4. Deglaze with sherry and flambé.
5. Add mint and ginger; then, after 30 seconds, add onions and red bell peppers. Add black bean garlic sauce and chicken stock.
6. Let simmer for at least 3 minutes, stirring all ingredients.
7. Serve over jasmine rice (also good with white or brown rice).

FISH AND SEAFOOD

The scent of garlic is the aroma of great food to come.

Bob Kinkead

"FISH" CHILI WITH LOTS OF GARLIC

Jerome Alden

Ingredients:

6 garlic cloves (or even more), peeled

1 each: red pepper, green pepper, yellow pepper, all washed and seeded

1 medium-sized onion, peeled

1/2 pound medium-sized shrimp, peeled and deveined

1 pound whitefish (cod, haddock, or flounder, etc.)

1 large can chopped tomatoes

2 tablespoons chili powder (or more to taste)

2 tablespoons cumin

2 or 3 cans (15.5 ounces) black beans, drained and rinsed

1 tablespoon each, dried: oregano, basil, dill

2 tablespoons Dijon mustard

a splash of lime juice

dry white wine as needed

3 to 4 tablespoons extra virgin olive oil

Throw the garlic, onion, and red, green, and yellow peppers into the food processor. Chop them not too fine so there's some "body" to this mirepoix. (Of course, you can also do this by hand.)

Cut each shrimp into thirds. Cut the fish into 1/4-inch chunks. Put them into a bowl and keep in the refrigerator until ready to finish the chili.

Pour some oil into the pot and heat. When the oil is hot enough, pour in the mirepoix. Cook, stirring, until the vegetables begin to soften.

Add the cumin, chili powder, oregano, basil. Mix together for 30 seconds so the flavors open up and blend.

Pour in 2 cups of white wine and stir. Add the lime juice, mustard, and dill. Stir to blend. Taste to make sure it has the "chili" flavor and "heat" you want.

Pour the beans into the pot. Stir. Bring to a boil. Then turn down the fire so the chili barely bubbles. Cook for about 30 minutes to give the flavors time to "marry" and the chili to thicken—tasting now and then to correct the flavors.

About 3 minutes before you're ready to serve, stir in the shrimp and fish. If the chili is too thick, add enough wine to make it work for you.

Serve in a bowl . . . on a lettuce leaf with rice on the side . . . or over rice.

(You can prepare the part without the fish an hour or two ahead. Let it sit with pot covered. Bring it back to bubbling before you add the shrimp and fish to finish.)

GARLIC-CRUSTED SNAPPER
WITH GRILLED GULF SHRIMP

Sam R. Bei and Regina Bonanno
Hudson's Ribs and Fish
Fishkill, New York

Ingredients for Grilled Shrimp:
12 jumbo shrimp
1 tablespoon crushed garlic
2 tablespoons fresh rosemary
juice of 2 lemons
7 ounces dark beer
2 ounces Worcestershire sauce
salt and pepper to taste

Mix all of the above together. Marinate shrimp in refrigerator for 2 hours.

Ingredients for Crusted Fish:
1 pound (4 fillets) of any light, flaky fish, such as pompano, grouper, tilapia, orange roughy
3 egg whites

1 head garlic, cloves peeled
4 ounces flour
2 ounces each, fresh: thyme, rosemary, parsley
salt and pepper to taste

Whisk egg whites until firm, set aside. Process garlic in food processor until finely chopped. Combine garlic with all herbs, salt and pepper, and flour. Dip fish in egg whites, then dredge in flour mixture. Set aside.

Ingredients for Basil Oil:
1 bunch fresh basil, thoroughly washed
3/4 cup extra virgin olive oil
salt and pepper to taste

Puree basil in blender with olive oil and salt and pepper to taste.

Sauté fish on both sides until golden brown and cooked through. While fish is cooking, grill or sauté shrimp.

Place fish on plate, top with shrimp skewered with a sprig of fresh rosemary. Drizzle with basil oil.

BAKED FISH WITH WALNUT-CORIANDER CHUTNEY

Walnut Marketing Board

Ingredients for 6 servings:
1-1/2 cups coriander leaves
3/4 cup walnut pieces
5 tablespoons lemon juice
3 cloves garlic, coarsely chopped
1 jalapeño pepper, seeded and coarsely chopped (about 3 inches long)
salt to taste
6 pieces (6 ounces each) swordfish or tuna or rock cod
toasted walnut pieces as garnish

In container of an electric blender combine coriander, 3/4 cup walnut pieces, lemon juice, garlic, and jalapeño. Blend to make a rough paste, pulsating blender on and off and scraping sides, as needed. Mix in salt.

*Arrange fish in shallow baking pan. Spread walnut mix-
ture on fish. Bake in preheated oven at 400 degrees just
until fish is opaque, 5 to 10 minutes.*
    Garnish with toasted walnuts. Serve with potatoes.

MACARONI SALMON LOAF

Gloria Rose
Cooking for Good Health
(Avery Publishing Group, 1993)

Ingredients for 4 servings:
4 ounces elbow macaroni, cooked al dente
1 can (1 pound) pink or red salmon
2 garlic cloves, minced
2 tablespoons onion, finely minced
1 tablespoon chopped parsley
dash of pepper
1 cup coarse whole wheat bread crumbs
3 egg whites
3/4 cup skim milk
1 teaspoon dried dill
1/4 teaspoon dried rosemary

1. Preheat oven to 350 degrees. Spray a 9-by-5-inch loaf pan
   with nonstick cooking spray.
2. Combine all ingredients in a medium-sized bowl with a
   fork.
3. Place in loaf pan and bake 35 to 40 minutes.

Variation:

*Heat 1/2 cup Marinara sauce with 2 tablespoons low-fat
buttermilk. Use as a sauce for salmon loaf.*

NUTRITIONAL BREAKDOWN (PER SERVING WITHOUT SAUCE)

Calories......................245
Protein ....25 g
Carbohydrates ....29 g

Fat.............................5 g
Sodium.......................444 mg
Cholesterol ....36 mg

LINGUINE WITH TUNA

Irena Chalmers

Ingredients for 4 servings:
2 large red bell peppers
3 tablespoons pine nuts
1/4 cup olive oil
8 ounces fresh tuna
4 medium-sized cloves garlic, chopped
1 medium-sized red onion, chopped
1/4 tablespoon hot red pepper flakes
1 tablespoon fresh chopped marjoram
2 tablespoons lemon juice
1 tablespoon capers
3 tablespoons chopped parsley
12 ounces linguine
salt

If using fresh peppers, heat the broiler and broil them until charred. Put them in a bowl and cover lightly with plastic wrap. When cool enough to handle, stem, seed, and peel them. Cut the peppers into small pieces.

Bring a large pot of water to the boil for the pasta.

Heat a 10-inch frying pan (without oil) over medium-high heat. Add the pine nuts and cook, shaking the pan for about 2 minutes until the nuts are lightly browned. Remove the nuts.

Reduce the heat to medium and add the oil to the frying pan. Sear the tuna for 2 minutes on each side. Chill the tuna quickly in the freezer for about 10 minutes, then slice it into strips.

Add the garlic, onion, and red pepper flakes to the hot oil. Stir-fry for about 4 minutes until softened. Add the roasted peppers. Add the fresh marjoram, lemon juice, capers, and parsley.

Add salt to the boiling water and cook the pasta for 10 minutes.

Drain the linguine. Add the pepper mixture, pine nuts, and sliced tuna.

PRAWNS SPANISH STYLE

Judy Knapp
Pikled Garlik Company
Pacific Grove, California

Ingredients for 3 to 4 servings:
2 tablespoons extra virgin olive oil
10 whole garlic cloves, peeled
1 pound unpeeled shrimp (size: 25 to 30 to a pound)
1 lemon
salt

Heat a griddle or heavy pan with oil until it is very hot. Begin cooking the garlic. When the cloves are browned, but not burned, remove and set aside.

Cook the shrimp on the hot surface, first one side and then the other, salting each side generously. When pinky-brown, approximately 5 minutes, place on serving dish, and toss with the garlic. Squeeze lemon juice over all.

Each person peels the shrimp themselves.

PASTA

*My Italian mother taught me two things to live by: guilt and garlic! Fortunately it is the latter that has had the most influence on my life. I learned to cook from watching both my mother and grandmother in the kitchen. One of the lessons I learned was **never** use an exact measurement but rather to add "some of this" and "a little bit of that." But the greatest revelation I stumbled upon was that there is actually only one Italian recipe in the world. First, you start with a seasoned skillet (that means it has years of black* *schmutz on it). Second, you sauté a "little" garlic in "some" olive oil. And finally, you add the rest of the ingredients. It works every time. But one word of caution: eating your delectable garlic-charged dish can induce incredible guilt!*

Steve Sorrentino

PASTA PRIMAVERA

Sandra Woodruff
Secrets of Fat-Free Cooking
(Avery Publishing Group, 1995)

Ingredients for 5 servings:
2-1/2 teaspoons cornstarch
1/4 teaspoon ground white pepper
1-1/2 cups evaporated skim milk
8 ounces spaghetti or fettuccine pasta
2 teaspoons crushed fresh garlic
1/2 cup thinly sliced carrots
1/2 cup sliced fresh mushrooms
2 cups fresh broccoli florets
1/2 small red bell pepper, cut into thin strips
1 medium onion, cut into thin wedges
1/2 cup plus 2 tablespoons grated nonfat or reduced-fat
  Parmesan cheese

1. Combine the cornstarch, pepper, and milk in a jar with a tight-fitting lid and shake until the cornstarch has dissolved. Set aside.
2. Cook the pasta al dente according to package directions. Drain well, return the pasta to the pot, and cover to keep warm.
3. Coat a large skillet with nonstick cooking spray. Place over medium-high heat, add the garlic, and stir-fry for 30 seconds. Add the vegetables along with 1 tablespoon of water. Cover and cook, stirring occasionally, for 3 to 5 minutes,

or until the vegetables are crisp-tender. Add a little more water if the skillet becomes too dry.

4. Reduce the heat to medium, and add the pasta to the skillet mixture. Shake the milk mixture, and add it to the skillet. Toss gently over medium heat for about 2 minutes, or just until the sauce begins to boil and thicken slightly.

5. Remove the skillet from the heat, and add the Parmesan. Toss gently to mix, and serve immediately.

NUTRIENTS PER 1-1/2 CUP SERVING

Calories.........................291
Protein ....17 g
Fat................................1.1 g
Cholesterol ....10 mg
Fiber ....3.2 g
Sodium........................194 mg

PASTA WITH ZUCCHINI AND ROASTED GARLIC

The National Pasta Association

Ingredients to serve 4:
1 pound pasta: Rotini, Twists, or Spirals—uncooked
8 medium cloves garlic, peeled
1/2 teaspoon dried thyme
1/2 teaspoon dried rosemary, crushed
2 tablespoons vegetable oil
3 medium zucchini, coarsely grated (about 5 or 6 cups)
salt and pepper to taste

Preheat oven or toaster oven to 450 degrees. Lay a 12-inch square piece of foil on the counter and put the garlic on it. Sprinkle thyme and rosemary over the garlic. Pour the oil over garlic and herbs. Draw up the edges of the foil and make a sealed packet. Bake 20 minutes.

While the garlic is baking, cook pasta according to package directions. Two minutes before pasta is done, add the zucchini to the pasta cooking water. Cook 2 minutes. Drain zucchini and pasta.

Open the foil and mash the garlic lightly with a spoon. Toss with the pasta and zucchini, season with salt and pepper and serve.

NUTRIENTS PER SERVING

Calories 477
Protein.................................. 15.5 g
Fat .... 9 g
Calories from Fat.................. 17 percent
Cholesterol .... 0 mg
Carbohydrates...................... 84.2 g
Sodium
  (before seasoning to taste).. 9.3 mg

PASTA HOPPIN' JOHN

The National Pasta Association

Ingredients for 6 to 8 servings:

1 pound Bow Ties, Wagon Wheels, or other medium pasta shape, uncooked

1 tablespoon vegetable oil

1 medium onion, chopped

1 jalapeño pepper, seeded and chopped or 1/2 teaspoon dried jalapeño flakes

3 cloves garlic, chopped

1 green bell pepper, seeded and chopped

1 can (28 ounces) crushed tomatoes

1 package (10 ounces) frozen black-eyed peas, prepared according to directions, or 1 can (16 ounces) black-eyed peas, rinsed and drained

1 tablespoon apple cider vinegar

3 tablespoons chopped fresh cilantro, or 1 tablespoon dried cilantro

salt and black pepper to taste

Cook pasta according to package directions; drain. In large sauté pan, heat oil over medium heat. Sauté the onion, jalapeño, garlic, and pepper until softened, about 3 minutes. Add tomatoes. Simmer 10 minutes partially covered. Stir occasionally. Add the black-eyed peas, vinegar, and cilantro. Cover and simmer an additional 10 minutes. Season with salt and black pepper. Toss gently with cooked pasta and serve immediately.

NUTRIENTS PER SERVING

Calories..................... 347
Protein .... 11.4 g
Fat............................. 3.64 g
Calories from Fat....... 9 percent
Cholesterol .... 0 mg
Carbohydrates .... 67 g
Sodium..................... 194 mg

ITALIAN ZITI BAKE

The National Pasta Association

Ingredients for 6 servings:
1 pound Ziti, Rigatoni, or other medium pasta shape, uncooked
1 teaspoon vegetable oil
1 large onion, chopped
2 medium zucchini, diced
3 cloves garlic, minced
1 can (28 ounces) crushed tomatoes in purée
2 teaspoons Italian seasoning
1/4 teaspoon crushed red pepper flakes
1/4 teaspoon salt
1/8 teaspoon pepper
2 egg whites
1 container (15 ounces) part-skim ricotta cheese
2/3 cup part-skim mozzarella cheese, grated
1/3 cup grated Parmesan cheese

Prepare pasta according to package directions. While pasta is cooking, warm the vegetable oil in a large saucepan over medium-low heat. Add the onion, zucchini, and garlic. Cover the pan and cook until the vegetables are very soft, about 10 minutes. Season with salt and pepper. Combine tomatoes, Italian seasoning and red pepper flakes.

Preheat oven to 325 degrees. Blend together the egg whites and ricotta cheese until smooth.

In a 3-quart casserole, layer the pasta, ricotta cheese, and tomato mixture, ending with a layer of the tomato mixture. Sprinkle the top with grated mozzarella and Parmesan cheese. Bake until golden brown on top and bubbling, about 45 minutes.

NUTRIENTS PER SERVING

Calories	648
Protein	31.4 g
Fat	12.4 g
Calories from Fat	17 percent
Cholesterol	33.5 mg
Carboyhdrates	103 g
Sodium	700 mg

SOUPS

L'aigo bouido sauvo la vido. (Garlic soup saves lives.)

Provençal saying translated by John Thorne

COLD GARLIC SOUP

Ted Matern
Dean & Deluca
New York, New York

Ingredients:
4 whole garlic bulbs
1 quart chicken stock

5 slices white bread with crusts removed
1/2 cup heavy cream
8 to 10 chives (garlic chives if available) finely chopped
salt and freshly ground pepper to taste

Blanch the garlic bulbs in boiling water, remove and peel all the cloves. Bring the chicken stock to a boil, add the garlic cloves and simmer for 15 to 20 minutes. Remove from the heat and add the bread slices. Put the soup in a food processor and process for 20 seconds. (This may be done in several small batches.) Return the processed soup to the pan and put back on the heat. Add the cream and simmer for 5 minutes. Allow to cool. Before serving, fully chill. Since it will have separated, mix well with a wire whisk.

Garnish with chopped chives.

SOPA DE AJO (GARLIC SOUP)

Jimmy Sanz

Restaurateur Jimmy Sanz has been serving this famous garlic soup for 26 years at Tio Pepe in New York City.

Ingredients per serving:
2 teaspoons minced garlic
2 tablespoons olive oil
1/4 teaspoon paprika
1-1/2 cups chicken broth
1/8 teaspoon minced parsley
1 egg
croutons
salt to taste

In a small pan, gently sauté garlic in oil until golden brown. Add croutons, lightly toasting, followed by paprika. Combine chicken broth, parsley, and without breaking the egg, add it, too. Bring to a boil. Carefully transfer to an appropriate soup bowl and serve immediately.

GARLIC SOUP

Diane Wilen

Ingredients:
3 cups vegetable broth
1 head garlic, peeled
2 potatoes, cubed
1-1/2 cups chopped carrots
1/2 cup evaporated milk and 1/2 cup water (combined)
pepper to taste
hot sauce to taste

Simmer first 4 ingredients, covered, for 20 minutes. Puree in food processor. Season with pepper and hot sauce, and add enough of the milk mixture to reach your idea of the perfect soup consistency. Heat and serve with croutons.

GARLIC CHOWDER

The Stinking Cookbook
The Stinking Rose, A Garlic Restaurant
San Francisco and Los Angeles

We've made this dish a true "family affair"—the *Allium* family, that is. Along with the savory onions, leeks, and, of course, garlic, the *Allium* family also includes about 600 bulb-like relatives and in-laws. (Wow, that must be one heck of a family portrait!)

Well, these three major family members, who get along most famously, have joined hands and tastes here to help us create a creamy, fragrant chowder that will be well received at *your* next family get-together.

Ingredients to serve 6 to 8:
2 ounces olive oil
optional: 4 ounces bacon, diced
2 medium onions, diced
1/2 head celery, diced

1 bunch fresh leeks, cleaned and chopped

5 heads roasted garlic (see Index for Roasted Garlic recipes)

2 tablespoons fresh thyme

3 medium potatoes, peeled and diced

6 cups chicken stock

salt and white pepper to taste

optional: 1 cup heavy cream

1/2 cup chopped fresh parsley

1. In a large pot, heat the olive oil.
2. Sauté the bacon and add the onions, celery, and leeks.
3. Remove the roasted garlic cloves from the head by squeezing the roasted head. Add roasted garlic pulp to the pot.
4. Add thyme, potatoes, and chicken stock.
5. Bring to a simmer and cook until potatoes are tender (about 30 minutes).
6. Season with salt and pepper.
7. Add cream and parsley. Remove from heat and serve.

LONG BEACH GARLIC BEEF SOUP

Northwest Garlic Festival
Ocean Park, Washington

Ingredients:

1/2 cup cooking oil

1 pound beef, cut in 1/2-inch cubes

1/4 teaspoon pepper

1/2 cup carrot, grated

1/2 cup celery, thin slices

6 tablespoons beef bouillon

1 tablespoon Kitchen Bouquet (flavoring)

water, at least 6 cups

1 cup fresh garlic, sliced

1 cup onions, chopped fine

1/2 cup flour

1/2 cup cooking oil

1/2 cup long-grain rice

optional garnish: garlic croutons, grated cheese, parsley

In 5-quart pot, heat oil on medium fire; add beef and pep-
per and stir for a few minutes. Then add carrot and celery
on top of meat, and add beef bouillon along with Kitchen
Bouquet and 2 cups water. Stir for a few minutes. Cover
pot, turn heat to low and simmer while preparing other
ingredients.

Heat oil in skillet on medium fire, then add onions and
garlic; fry till brown. Add flour; stir and cook a few min-
utes to cook flour, then set aside.

Add rice and 4 cups water to cooking meat pot and stir
well. Cover again and keep cooking for an hour or two,
until meat is very tender. Stir garlic and onion mixture
into soup pot a little at a time, mixing well. Cover. Add
more water as needed; continue cooking for about 30 min-
utes on low.

Serve hot; sprinkle grated cheese and parsley on top.
Great with hot garlic croutons on top or hot garlic French
bread.

TOMATO AND RISOTTO BISQUE

Florida Tomato Committee

Ingredients for 10 servings:

10 fresh ripe (Florida) tomatoes, roughly diced

2 tablespoons olive oil

6 cloves garlic, minced

1 medium Spanish onion, diced small

1 cup celery, diced small

1-1/2 quarts vegetable stock or water

1-1/4 cups uncooked risotto rice

1 or 2 tablespoons cinnamon (to taste)

salt and pepper to taste

1. Sauté garlic, onion, and celery in olive oil. Add tomatoes,
   sauté 3 minutes.

2. Add stock, bring to a boil, add rice, simmer 1-1/2 hours. Stir occasionally.

3. When rice is cooked in soup, purée in blender or food processor. Strain and add seasonings. Simmer 20 minutes and adjust seasonings and consistency to taste.

SPREADS, SAUCES, DIPS, DRESSINGS, AND A RUB

SALSA DI MOLTO AGLIO

Balducci's
New York, New York

Forty cloves of garlic sounds like a lot, but you'd never guess there's that much in this dish. The unsalted butter, whole milk, salty anchovies, and acidic tomatoes conspire to tone the garlic's pungency down and coax its mellow sweetness. People who taste this sauce swoon over every bite without knowing what makes it so satisfying. Maybe it's best not to tell them.

Emily Balducci

Ingredients for 4 cups of sauce over 1 pound of pasta:
3/4 cup olive oil
40 cloves garlic, minced very finely into a paste
1 heaping tablespoon anchovy paste
14 large, ripe plum tomatoes, seeded and diced
1/4 teaspoon sugar
1/4 cup freshly chopped basil
1/2 cup sweet butter
1/2 cup whole milk
1/2 teaspoon salt
1/4 teaspoon freshly ground black pepper
2 tablespoons freshly grated Parmigiano Reggiano

Heat a thick-bottomed skillet over high heat for 2 minutes. Add olive oil and garlic at the same time and cook about 1 to 2 minutes, shaking pan continuously, until garlic is just turning gold. Add anchovy paste and continue cooking, stirring, until anchovy paste dissolves, about 1 minute more. Add tomatoes and sugar and cook another 3 minutes, stirring and smashing tomatoes so they dissolve. Add basil and cook about 1 more minute. Add butter and let melt, then add milk, salt, and pepper. Cook another minute, still stirring continuously. Remove pan from heat and pour sauce over al dente pasta. Sprinkle cheese on top, stir gently, and serve.

Nina Balducci recommends serving this sauce over a chunky, extruded pasta such as penne rigate, mezzi rigatoni, or fusilli. You could also stir into steamed rice or spoon on pizza crust or toasted slabs of peasant bread.

GARLIC LOVERS' PASTA DELIGHT

Jerome Alden

Simple. And in its own way: garlic-elegance . . . especially when serving pasta as a side dish.

Try it for two people . . . expand the ingredients to serve more.

6 to 8 cloves garlic finely chopped
1 cup extra virgin olive oil

Put the oil into a small pot. Put the garlic into oil. Stir to mix well. Light the burner and bring to a boil.

Then turn off the burner. Put a top on the pot. And let the garlic steep until you've cooked the pasta and are ready to serve. If it's cold, just reheat and pour it over the pasta.

You could add Parmesan cheese.

You could add parsley.

You could add fresh ground pepper.

You could add . . .

*I put garlic in practically everything I can think of,
except desserts. I don't know how people who dislike
it exist.*

James Beard

JAMES BEARD'S RED PEPPER
GARLIC PASTA SAUCE

Jerome Alden

Jim Beard was an old good friend and of course an even older
and good lover of garlic. One day my wife, Barbara, and I were
visiting him in his 12th Street house in New York City, and as
we walked through his kitchen I noticed four or five luxurious
looking red peppers on the counter next to a head of garlic.

"What're you gonna do with those?" I asked.

"Make a pasta sauce for dinner tonight," he answered.

"How?"

"Roast the peppers. Remove the skins. Purée them in the
Cuisinart." (Remember, he practically introduced that smart
device to the USA.) "With a lot of garlic."

"That's it?" I asked. "No oil?"

"Yes, of course. Enough olive oil dripped through the
funnel to bind it." "And that's it?"

"Well, I chop some onions and add them raw just before
I toss the sauce over the cooked pasta."

Of course, Barbara and I rushed out of there to the near-
est store . . . bought some fresh garlic, red peppers, and an
onion . . . and that night had our own pasta with a very easy,
unusual, and very tasty sauce.

That night I used 2 red peppers, 4 cloves of garlic, half
an onion. I've since used 1 jar of roasted red peppers . . . it
seems to work just as well.

I don't know if James Beard ever heated it up before
serving. I do now and then, and it's great!!!

PIPERADE/SPANISH SAUCE FOR EGGS

American Egg Board

In the western Pyrenees, the Basques scramble a zestily flavored vegetable mixture right in with the eggs for a dish called
Piperade. Use the same thick sauce to top off Spanish omelets
or scrambled, fried, or poached eggs with pizzazz. For a
Creole twist, add chopped celery and a touch of liquid hot
pepper sauce.

Ingredients for about 1-1/2 cups:
1 can (16 ounces) tomatoes, undrained
1/2 cup chopped green pepper
1/2 cup chopped onion
1 to 2 cloves garlic, minced
Poached or scrambled or fried eggs or omelets

*Place tomatoes, pepper, onion, and garlic in small
saucepan. Stir to break up tomatoes. Cook over medium
heat, stirring occasionally, until liquid evaporates, about
20 minutes. Spoon over your favorite cooked eggs.*

UNCOOKED TOMATO SAUCE FOR PASTA

"Garlicfest"
Fairfield, Connecticut

Ingredients for 4 to 6 servings:
4 large, ripe tomatoes at room temperature
1/2 cup pitted sliced ripe olives
1/2 cup chopped fresh basil or 1 tablespoon dried basil
4 or more garlic cloves, squeezed through garlic press
1/4 teaspoon red pepper flakes
salt and freshly ground pepper to taste
1/2 cup olive oil
1 pound vermicelli (or any pasta you prefer)
optional: Parmesan cheese

*Chop tomatoes and place in large glass or plastic bowl.
Add olives, herbs, spices, and salt and pepper, and mix
well. Add olive oil and toss together. Allow sauce to stand
at room temperature several hours to blend flavors. Sauce
may be refrigerated overnight but should be returned to
room temperature before serving. Cook pasta and drain.
Add tomato sauce and toss gently. Serve immediately.
Grated Parmesan cheese may be added to the pasta before
serving.*

AIR FORCE ONE'S SECRET APPLESAUCE

Clipper Mill
San Francisco, California

Ingredients:
2 cups applesauce
1 garlic clove, crushed
1 tablespoon horseradish

*Mix all ingredients and refrigerate. Serve with roast or
barbequed pork.*

GARLIC MARMALADE

Marilou Robinson
Northwest Garlic Festival

Ingredients:
2 cups peeled garlic, finely chopped
1/3 cup olive oil
1/2 cup chicken broth
1 cup orange marmalade

*Cook ingredients over medium heat, stirring occasionally,
till liquid is reduced and mixture thickens to consistency
of thick ketchup. Cool; refrigerate covered. Marmalade
keeps very well in refrigerator (do not keep it longer than 2
weeks), and may even be frozen.
    Can be used instead of cranberry sauce with turkey, or
instead of mint jelly with lamb.*

SKORDALIA

Sylvia Panagos

Ingredients:
4 medium-sized potatoes, peeled and diced
1 bulb garlic, cloves separated and peeled
1 cup Cream of Rice (uncooked)
1 cup white vinegar
1 cup canola oil (olive oil tends to be a bit heavy for this
   recipe)

*Press garlic cloves into mixer bowl and start mixer on
slow. Place potatoes in 4 cups water and bring to a boil.
When potatoes are fork-tender, remove from water (save
the potato water) and place potatoes into the mixer bowl
with the garlic, and continue on slow. Add about 1/2 cup
water to the potato water and bring to boil, then add
Cream of Rice. Cook and stir over medium heat for about a
minute until the Cream of Rice is cooked. Take off the heat
and carefully add to the mixer bowl. As the mixture is
blending the ingredients, slowly blend in the oil and vinegar on an alternating basis—2 tablespoons oil, 2 tablespoons vinegar. Keep blending both until nothing remains.*

*It's great on bread, melba toast, crackers, baked fish,
and veggies.*

*If any Skordalia is left over (which is unusual with this
delicious dish) it can be stored in a jar in the refrigerator.
Do not keep it longer than 2 weeks.*

PRESTO PESTO

(Multi-Use Garlic Pesto Sauce)

Arlen Hollis Kane

Ingredients:
1 bunch fresh basil
6 ounces shelled walnuts or almonds
1/4 cup finely grated Parmesan cheese
4 large cloves garlic, peeled
extra virgin olive oil

*Wash basil leaves well in cold water and dry thoroughly.
In a food processor, combine the basil, walnuts, and garlic.
Process until near purée consistency. Add Parmesan cheese
and process again until ingredients are well integrated
(about 5 seconds). While processing, use the funnel to add
enough olive oil to moisten the mixture. The purée should
be like a paste, not wet or shiny.*

This garlic-enhanced pesto can be:

- spread on toasted French or Italian bread
- added to fresh or canned tomatoes and heated to use as pesto pasta sauce
- spread (1 or 2 tablespoons) on broiled fish or chicken for a fast gourmet touch
- used as a sandwich spread for a Mediterranean taste treat
- added to balsamic vinegar with a bit more olive oil and used as salad dressing
- tossed with rice, or any steamed vegetable as a side dish
- mashed into mashed potatoes, or as a topping on a baked potato

*The flavor of Presto Pesto is so intense that only a small
amount is needed to make a dish spark. As a result, it can
turn low-fat, bland foods (such as scrod) into gourmet fare
while keeping the additional fat grams in line.*

*Leftover pesto should be refrigerated. Do not keep it
longer than 2 weeks.*

GUACAMOLE

Katharine Kagel
Cafe Pasqual's Cookbook
(Chronicle Books, 1993)

In the Southwest, guacamole is always in demand. Indeed, all of America is now aware of this classic *mole*. At Cafe Pasqual's we serve it as a topping on burritos and as a filling in quesadillas and omelets. But it is also wonderful served simply as a dip for yellow corn tortilla chips or raw vegetables such as jicama, bell pepper, or celery strips.

Superb guacamole depends on perfectly ripe and flavorful ingredients. Undoubtedly, you will have to make adjustments for the condition of the available avocados and tomatoes. Avocados are ripe when they yield to gentle fingertip pressure. The black, bumpy-skinned Haas variety is preferred because of its rich flavor. In winter, the smooth-skinned Fuertes avocado from Florida is widely available, but it is difficult to make great guacamole from it. If you must use the Fuertes variety, add extra lime juice, a bit of olive oil to offset its watery nature, and use the ripest Italian plum tomatoes you can find.

Guacamole should be mixed using only hand implements. An old-fashioned hand-held potato masher works well, leaving appetizing little chunks of avocado, tomato, and onion to please the tastebuds.

Ingredients:

3 large, fully ripe avocados, peeled and pitted

1 tomato, seeded and finely diced

1/3 white onion, finely diced

optional: 1 fresh jalapeño chile or 1/2 fresh serrano chile, stemmed, seeded, and finely minced

3 cloves garlic, finely minced

salt

optional: freshly ground black pepper

juice of 3 limes or 2 lemons

In a large bowl, mash the avocados with a fork, potato masher, or other hand implement until the mixture is generally smooth, but with some chunks left for texture.

Add the tomato, onion, and the chile, if using, and mix thoroughly. Season with the garlic and with salt and pepper to taste. Use a mortar and pestle, if you have one, to blend these seasoning ingredients before adding them. Add the lime or lemon juice and mix well.

Serve the guacamole within 2 hours of preparing it. To store guacamole, press plastic wrap directly onto its surface to prevent the discoloration that occurs from contact with air, and place in the refrigerator. Serve at room temperature.

BAGNA CALDA

Lester Mestas
Granito Piedre Grille, A Garlic Restaurant
Rocklin, California

In my neighborhood, this classic Italian dish was especially popular around Christmastime. We used to eat tons of it with sourdough bread.

Ingredients for 4 to 6 servings:
2 cups large peeled garlic cloves
3/4 cup extra virgin olive oil
4 ounces salted butter
1 can (2 ounces) anchovies
salt and pepper to taste

Chop anchovies fine and place all ingredients in an oven casserole. Salt and pepper to taste. Cover with foil and place in 325-degree oven for 1-1/2 hours.
    Serve with good sourdough, Italian, or French bread. It tastes even better if you eat with people you love.

PARSLEY-GARLIC DIP AND SPREAD

Robert Pardi

Ingredients:
1 bunch finely chopped parsley
3 large garlic cloves, finely minced
1 cup mayonnaise or yogurt or sour cream or whipped
    cream cheese (nonfat of any of these works fine)

Combine all ingredients and refrigerate until ready to use. Tastes great on pita, crackers, chips, or veggies (celery, carrots, cukes, etc.). Can also be used as a mixture for egg or tuna salad.

REDUCED FAT (EGGLESS) CAESAR DRESSING

The Garlic Information Center
New York Hospital-Cornell University Medical Center

Ingredients for 10 servings (1 serving = 2 tablespoons):
3 heads roasted garlic (directions following)
juice of 2 lemons
olive oil
2 teaspoons mustard
3 tablespoons balsamic vinegar
1 teaspoon pepper
1/2 teaspoon salt
2 anchovy fillets
1/2 cup water
2 tablespoons Parmesan cheese

Purée mustard, salt, anchovy fillets, lemon juice, water, balsamic vinegar, and roasted garlic heads in the food processor. Slowly drizzle in olive oil until well emulsified. Season with salt and add Parmesan cheese.

NUTRIENTS PER SERVING

Protein .... 1 g
Fat .... 6 g (70 percent)
Carbohydrates .... 4 g
Sodium .... 175 mg
Calories 76

ROASTED GARLIC

Ingredients:
4 heads of garlic
1/2 cup chicken stock

Preheat oven to 350 degrees. Remove outer papery skin from garlic heads, leaving the whole head intact. Arrange garlic heads in a small baking dish. Pour chicken stock over the garlic, cover tightly with foil and bake for about an hour (add a little more chicken stock or water if needed). Uncover and bake for 15 more minutes. Remove from the oven and let cool.

GARLIC HERB (FAT-FREE) SALAD DRESSING

James Levin, M.D., and Natalie Cederquist
A Vegetarians Ecstasy
(Avery Publishing Group, 1990)

A wonderful no-oil fat-free vinaigrette. Use as a marinade for vegetables.

Ingredients for about 2-1/2 cups:
2 cups filtered water
1/4 teaspoon agar flakes (available in health food stores)
5 tablespoons balsamic or cider vinegar
1-1/2 tablespoons garlic, chopped
2 green onions, chopped
2 teaspoons onion powder
1 teaspoon each: coriander, basil, oregano
1/2 teaspoon cracked black pepper
1 teaspoon barley malt syrup or honey

1. Dissolve the agar in the filtered water then transfer to a pot. Bring the agar-water mixture to a boil for 1 minute then pour it into a blender.
2. Add the rest of the ingredients, blend, and refrigerate. Whisk before serving.

GARLIC VINAIGRETTE

Clipper Mill
San Francisco, California

Ingredients:
4 large garlic cloves, minced
2 tablespoons Dijon mustard

1/3 cup red wine vinegar
1 cup extra virgin olive oil
salt and pepper to taste

Mix well and serve on salad. If any is left over, be sure to refrigerate.

CREAMY VINAIGRETTE

Clipper Mill
San Francisco, California

Ingredients:
2 garlic cloves, minced or crushed
1/2 cup olive oil
2 tablespoons balsamic vinegar
1/2 teaspoon salt
2 tablespoons yogurt
1 tablespoon mayonnaise
1/2 teaspoon dried basil
1/4 teaspoon dried dill
1/4 teaspoon dried thyme

Mix and refrigerate until ready to use.

RON'S RUB

Ronald E. Franzmeier

Ingredients for 3-1/4 cups:
1/2 cup chili powder
1 cup garlic powder
1 cup onion powder
1/2 cup paprika
1/4 cup salt

Mix all ingredients together in a bowl and "rub" the mixture all over the surface of the food—beef, chicken, or fish (for vegetables, cover with a thin layer of oil before using the "rub")—then let it stand for at least 45 minutes at

*room temperature before grilling fish fillets, and at least an
hour for meat and poultry.*
  Put leftover "rub" in a jar and refrigerate.

SWEET TREATS AND SNACKS

*With garlic, eating becomes an activity that involves
both the senses and the mind. The nose becomes
invigorated—it knows, the nose, precisely what it was
born to do, not just smell, but smell garlic. The palate
tingles in a way it had not tingled before, the insides
glow with satisfaction, the whole being of the human
animal is aware of new possibilities of enjoyment.
Eating suddenly turns into Art.*

Stanley Hoffman

HONEY-LUSCIOUS GARAPPLE PIE

Mrs. Vivienne Sommerset
Northwest Garlic Festival

Ingredients:
Crust for double 8-inch pie
5 or 6 Golden Delicious or Granny Smith apples, peeled and
  sliced thinly
20 cloves garlic, peeled and chopped finely
1/4 cup honey
1/4 cup hot water
1/4 teaspoon nutmeg
1/4 teaspoon cinnamon

*Into 8-inch pie pan lined with crust, put 1 layer of sliced
apples. Next, layer with 1/2 of chopped garlic. Add second
layer of apples and garlic. Sprinkle pie with spices. Mix
hot water and honey, saving a small amount to brush over
top crust; pour remainder into pie. Cover with top crust
and brush over with remaining bit of honey water. Bake
pie at 400 degrees for 15 minutes, and finish baking pie at
375 degrees for 50 to 60 minutes.*

GARLIC CHIP COOKIES

The Garlic Lovers Cookbook, Vols. I & II
The Gilroy Garlic Festival Association, Inc.

Ingredients for 5 dozen cookies:
10 cloves fresh garlic, unpeeled
boiling water
1/2 cup maple syrup
1 cup butter, softened
3/4 cup each: brown sugar, white sugar
2 eggs
1 teaspoon vanilla
1/2 teaspoon salt
2-1/4 cups chocolate chips
1/2 cup chopped nuts
2-1/2 cups flour
1 teaspoon baking soda

Drop garlic cloves into boiling water for about 5 minutes until tender. Peel and chop garlic and soak in maple syrup for 20 minutes.

Meanwhile, cream butter, sugars, eggs, and vanilla together until light and fluffy. Combine flour, baking soda, and salt. Add to cream mixture. Then stir in chocolate chips and nuts. Drain garlic and add to cookie batter. Blend well.

Drop cookie batter by tablespoon about 2 inches apart onto ungreased cookie sheet. Bake at 375 degrees for 8 to 10 minutes, until lightly browned. Remove from oven and cool on racks.

UNCLE RONNIE'S GARLIC CHEESECAKE

"Garlicfest"
Fairfield, Connecticut

Ingredients for 16 to 20 servings:
1-1/2 cups graham-cracker crumbs
2-3/4 cups sugar

1/4 teaspoon salt
3/4 cup light cream
juice of 1 lemon
1 ounce crushed garlic
3 pounds cream cheese
5 tablespoons cornstarch
1 dozen eggs
grated peel of 1 lemon
1/4 teaspoon vanilla

Reserve 1/2 cup of the crumbs. Press remaining crumbs onto bottom and 2 inches up the sides of generously-buttered 10-inch springform pan.

Stir cream cheese to soften; beat till fluffy. Mix sugar, cornstarch, and salt; gradually blend into cheese. Add eggs, one at a time, beating well after each. Be sure there are no lumps. Stir in remaining ingredients for filling.

Pour into the crumb-lined pan. Bake in 325-degree oven for 1 hour and 40 minutes, or till done. (Cake will not be completely set in center and will have slight depression on top.) Cool in pan for about 2 hours. Chill.

THE BIG FINISH

Garlic Ice Cream

The Stinking Cookbook
The Stinking Rose: A Garlic Restaurant
San Francisco and Los Angeles

Time and time again, patrons of The Stinking Rose look to this dessert selection on our menu and inquire, "Is there *really* garlic in the ice cream?" You bet there is! It's just the right amount to make our Garlic Ice Cream the most stinkingly good (and likely the most unusual) dessert you've ever tasted! It's also a really cool (and creamy) way to top off a delightfully garlicky meal.

Ingredients for 4 to 5 servings:
3 cups whole milk

1/4 teaspoon freshly chopped garlic
1 vanilla bean, split in half
1 cup heavy cream
1-1/2 cups granulated sugar
9 egg yolks

1. Put milk, garlic, and vanilla in a saucepan. Bring to a boil and remove from heat.
2. In a mixing bowl, blend cream, sugar, and egg yolks.
3. Strain the scalded milk mixture into the egg, cream and sugar mixture, stirring constantly.
4. Return the combined mixture to the pan and stir continuously over moderate heat until it coats the back of a spoon, about 10 to 15 minutes.
5. Cool in an ice bath.
6. Freeze until firm.

HOLIDAY GARLIC ICE CREAM

"Garlicfest"
Fairfield, Connecticut

After a spicy, rich dinner, this dessert is a refreshing climax. It should not be served after a bland, garlic-free meal, as the slight hint of garlic will be extremely offensive to some. The strawberry or other fruit topping can be eliminated, along with the sugar, and the resultant mixture can be served with roast beef in lieu of horseradish sauce.

Ingredients for 6 to 8 servings:
1 to 1-1/2 teaspoons gelatin
1/4 cup cold water
2 cups milk
3/4 to 1 cup sugar
1/8 teaspoon salt

2 tablespoons lemon juice
2 cloves garlic, minced
2 cups whipping cream
strawberry topping (or other fruit)

Soak the gelatin in cold water while you heat to a boil the milk, sugar, and salt. Dissolve the gelatin in the hot milk mixture. Cool, then add the lemon juice and garlic. Chill the mixture until slushy. Whip the cream until thick but not stiff, and stir into the mixture. Freeze in a mold or in a foil-covered tray. Top each portion with fresh fruit.

SICILIAN GEMS

The Garlic Lovers Cookbook, Vols. I & II
The Gilroy Garlic Festival Association, Inc.

Chocolate-coated garlic cloves? Why not! Margaret Buccery, the originator of the recipe, thinks that these little Sicilian Gems are a wonderful way to get your family to eat garlic and enjoy it.

Ingredients:
3 large garlic bulbs (about 30 cloves)
ice water
1/2 pound sweet dark chocolate
1 tablespoon Grand Marnier or liqueur of your choice
optional: ground walnuts

Separate and peel cloves of garlic. Soak in ice water to seal in flavor and juices while you are preparing the chocolate. Melt chocolate in double boiler or fondue pot; add liqueur and blend well. Dry garlic cloves and dip until completely covered in the chocolate-liqueur mixture. Allow to harden. (They may be rolled in ground nuts before they harden.)

Serve on a small, elegant dish at the end of the meal, along with cappuccino.

SAVORY WALNUT CRISPS

Walnut Marketing Board

Ingredients for about 3/4 cup spread, enough for 3 or 4 dozen crisps:

1/2 cup butter or margarine, softened
1/2 cup grated Parmesan cheese
1/4 cup finely chopped toasted walnuts
2 tablespoons chopped parsley
2 cloves garlic, pressed
thin slices baguette, toasted

In a small bowl mix butter, cheese, walnuts, parsley, and garlic until well blended. Spread each baguette slice with a thin layer of butter-walnut mixture. Arrange on baking sheet; broil until browned and bubbly, 1 or 2 minutes. Serve hot.
(Preparation time: 20 minutes.)

GARLIC POPCORN BALLS

Linda Tarvin
The Garlic Lovers Cookbook, Vols. I & II
Gilroy Garlic Festival Association, Inc.

Ingredients for 4 dozen popcorn balls:

50 cloves fresh garlic (about 4 heads)
2 teaspoons salt
4 cups shredded cheddar cheese (about 1 pound)
5 quarts popped corn (it takes about 1/2 cup unpopped corn)

Peel garlic and mince with salt to prevent sticking and to absorb garlic juices. Toss garlic with cheese.
In large glass bowl, make alternate layers of popped corn and garlic-cheese mixture, coating popcorn as evenly as possible, especially at edge of bowl.
Place in microwave oven and cook 1 minute. Shake bowl gently; turn 180 degrees and cook 1 more minute. Do

not overcook. Immediately turn out onto cookie sheet and quickly shape into plum-size balls. Set balls on sheets of waxed paper.

SUNFLOWER SNAPS

Camille Russell
The Garlic Lovers Cookbook, Vols. I & II
Gilroy Garlic Festival Association, Inc.

Ingredients:
1 tablespoon vegetable oil
2 cups raw sunflower seeds, shelled
8 cloves fresh garlic, minced
1/4 teaspoon salt
1 tablespoon soy sauce

Heat oil in large frying pan over medium-high heat. Add sunflower seeds and garlic. Stir. When a few of the seeds turn golden, reduce heat to medium, and continue stirring as needed. Stop cooking when about half the seeds are golden. Remove from heat and add salt. After 5 minutes add soy sauce and stir. Store in a jar with a tight lid.

Not only are they super as a snack, they also make a crunchy addition to salads, soups, hot cereal, and baked beans.

TOFU

Tomatoes and oregano make it Italian; wine and tarragon make it French. Sour cream makes it Russian; lemon and cinnamon make it Greek. Soy makes it Chinese; garlic makes it good.

Alice May Brock
Alice's Restaurant Cookbook

FRAGRANT PEPPERCORN TOFU

Martin Yan
Martin Yan's Culinary Journey Through China
(Yan Can Cook, Inc., KQED Books, 1995)

Ingredients for 4 servings:
1/2 pound lean ground chicken, pork, or beef
1 package (14 ounces) regular-firm tofu, drained
2 tablespoons cooking oil
tablespoon minced garlic
chopped green onions for garnish

Marinade
1 tablespoon oyster-flavored sauce
1 teaspoon cornstarch

Sauce
1/3 cup chicken broth
2 tablespoons soy sauce
1-1/2 teaspoons chili garlic sauce*
1 teaspoon black bean garlic sauce*
1 teaspoon cornstarch
1 teaspoon sugar
1/2 teaspoon ground toasted Sichuan peppercorns

1. Combine marinade ingredients in a bowl. Add meat and mix well. Let stand for 10 minutes. Cut tofu into 1/2-inch cubes. Combine sauce ingredients in a bowl; set aside.
2. Place a wok over high heat until hot. Add oil, swirling to coat sides. Add garlic and cook, stirring, until fragrant, about 10 seconds. Add meat and stir-fry for 2 minutes. Add tofu and sauce. Cook, stirring gently, until tofu is heated through and sauce boils and thickens. Place in a serving bowl and garnish with green onions.

*Available in Asian markets and some supermarkets.

NEW-AGE GUACAMOLE

Shea MacKenzie
The Garden of Earthly Delights
(Avery Publishing Group, 1993)

While I love good guacamole, I seldom have it, partly because of the inconsistencies of fresh avocados, but mostly because of the high fat content. Since this delicious low-fat dip does not depend on fresh ingredients, it is easily prepared even during the winter months. If you prefer a chunkier, less silky version, omit the tofu and double the amount of beans. Ideal as a dip with spicy tortilla chips, New Age Guacamole is also wonderful served with cheese, asparagus, and tofu fajitas.

Ingredients for 2 cups:

1 package (10 ounces) frozen baby lima beans, thawed
2/3 cup (5 ounces) silken tofu (if you have only firm tofu, add 1/3 cup part-skim farmer cheese and 1/4- to 1/2-cup yogurt to the blender)
2 cloves garlic, crushed
2-1/2 tablespoons fresh lemon juice
1 teaspoon sea salt
1/8 teaspoon crushed dried hot red chilies (or to taste)
1/2 jalapeño chili (or to taste), chopped
1/2 teaspoon cumin
1/2 teaspoon freshly ground black pepper
2 scallions (white parts only), chopped

1. In a small pot, cook the lima beans according to package directions. Drain and place in a blender or food processor with the tofu, garlic, lemon juice, salt, red chilies, jalapeño chili, cumin, and black pepper. Process until smooth.

2. Transfer the "guacamole" to an interesting-looking crock or bowl and stir in the scallions. Cover lightly and refrigerate for 1 hour.

3. Serve this dip with crackers, chips, crudites, or pieces of pita.

VEGETABLES

There is no such thing as a little garlic.

Arthur Baer
quote in *The Frank Muir Book*

RATATOUILLE

Alice Waters, Restaurateur and Author
Chez Panisse Vegetables (HarperCollins, 1996)

Garlic is so important at Chez Panisse (in Berkeley, California) that for the past 20 years we have had an annual garlic festival on Bastille Day, when virtually every dish is strongly flavored by *Allium sativum*, the stinking rose of the kitchen. Throughout the rest of the year it remains indispensable.

Ingredients to serve 8:
1 large eggplant
salt
3 onions
3 red bell peppers
4 summer squashes
5 tomatoes
6 to 12 cloves garlic
extra virgin olive oil
optional: hot pepper flakes
1 large bunch basil (about 1/2 pound)

Cut the eggplant into 1/2-inch cubes. Salt it liberally and leave it to drain in a colander.
Peel and cut up the onions, then the peppers, squashes, and tomatoes, keeping them all separate. Everything should be cut into pieces about the same size as the cubed eggplant. Smash and peel the garlic and chop it coarsely. Press down on the eggplant to extract more water and dry it.

In a heavy-bottomed pot, heat some of the olive oil and gently fry the eggplant until golden. Drain and reserve. Add more olive oil to the pot, and over medium-low heat start sautéing the onions. When they are soft and translucent, add the garlic, optional hot pepper flakes, and a bouquet garni consisting of the bunch of basil wrapped tightly with string, reserving a handful of the basil leaves for a garnish. Stir for a minute, toss in the peppers, and cook for a few minutes; next add the squash and cook a few minutes more, and then add the tomatoes. Cook for about 10 minutes, stirring occasionally. Finally add the eggplant and cook 15 to 25 minutes more, until everything is soft and the flavors have melded together. Remove the bouquet of basil, pressing on it to extract all its flavors, and adjust the seasoning with freshly chopped basil leaves, salt, and a bit of fresh extra virgin olive oil and finely chopped garlic, if needed. Serve warm or cold. The dish tastes even better the next day.

Note: Another method of making ratatouille is to fully cook all the vegetables separately, then combine them with the tomatoes, herbs, and seasonings just before serving. This makes for a very beautiful dish; the vegetables don't break down, and the shape and color of each remain intact.

CATALAN POTATOES

Bob Kinkead, Chef/Owner
Kinkead's
Washington, D.C.

These potatoes get a generous dose of garlic from both chopped garlic and garlic-infused oil. If you cook this dish in a nonstick pan, you can use less oil.

Ingredients to serves 6:

1/2 cup olive oil (1/3 cup for nonstick pans)

3 whole cloves garlic, peeled

1 large Spanish onion, diced

2 large Idaho potatoes (about 1 pound total), peeled and sliced 1/4-inch thick

3 cloves garlic, chopped fine
4 plum tomatoes, peeled, seeded, and diced
1 teaspoon salt; more to taste
1/2 teaspoon freshly ground black pepper; more to taste

Heat an 8- or 9-inch skillet over medium heat. Pour in the olive oil and add the whole garlic cloves. Cook the garlic until browned, about 8 minutes. Discard the cloves.

Add half the potato slices to the oil. Top them with an even layer of the onions, chopped garlic, tomatoes, salt, and pepper. Top with the remaining potato slices.

Cook the potatoes until browned, about 15 minutes, and then turn the potatoes over, pressing down on them with a spatula. (You don't have to turn all the potatoes at once; the potato cake will still keep its shape.)

Continue cooking until the underside is brown and the potatoes are tender throughout, about another 15 minutes. Slide from the pan onto a serving platter and serve immediately.

GARLIC MASHED POTATOES

Eileen Nock

Ingredients for 4 servings:
4 medium- to large-sized potatoes
3 bulbs of garlic
milk
butter
salt

Bake the potatoes and the whole, unpeeled garlic in a 400-degree oven for about an hour, or until the potatoes are done.

Cut the potatoes in half lengthwise and carefully scoop them out into a bowl, leaving the skins intact. Snip off the tops of the cloves and squish the garlic out of each clove into the bowl with the potatoes. If, in the process, little pieces of burnt garlic peel fall into the bowl, be sure to take them out. Add salt (a pinch per potato), then mix the potatoes, gradually adding butter and milk until you have a fluffy consistency.

Stuff the potato skins with the mixture and garnish according to your taste. Hot sauce and grated cheese—cheddar or Parmesan—are the most popular. Put the potatoes under the broiler for a couple of minutes, until the cheese begins to bubble. Serve hot.

NIÇOISE POTATOES

Luke David Schultheis
Director of Food and Beverage
Mayflower Hotel, New York, New York

Ingredients:

2 large potatoes
1 large bulb garlic, roasted (see Index for Roasted Garlic recipes)
2 tablespoons extra virgin olive oil
2 dry cured Greek black olives, chopped
1 ounce chopped sundried tomatoes
kosher (coarse) salt and coarse ground black pepper
milk
garnish: fresh marjoram or rosemary

Peel and cook potatoes until done. Drain liquid. Add roasted garlic pulp, milk, and salt and pepper to taste. Mash. Finish with tomatoes, olives, and olive oil.
　　Garnish with marjoram or rosemary.

MASHED SWEET POTATOES WITH GARLIC

Diane Wilen

Ingredients:

5 pounds yams (about 8), roasted
2 heads garlic, roasted
1 teaspoon olive oil
1 cup soy margarine
1 cup milk
3 cups vegetarian chicken broth (available at health food stores)

salt and pepper to taste

Cut the yams in half and, into a bowl, scoop out the pota-
toes from their skins. Squeeze the roasted garlic pulp into
the bowl and mash with olive oil. Add margarine, milk,
and enough broth to make yams a light consistency.
Season with salt and pepper.

MARINATED ARTICHOKES

California Artichoke Advisory Board

Ingredients for 6 to 8 servings:
3 quarts water
2 cups white vinegar
3 cloves garlic
1 teaspoon salt
24 California baby artichokes, trimmed to edible stage—
  keep whole
1 cup wine vinegar
1 cup vegetable oil
1/2 teaspoon garlic powder
3 tablespoons minced parsley

Bring water, white vinegar, garlic cloves, and salt to a
rolling boil. Stir in artichokes. Continue stirring for 1
minute. Cover and boil 10 to 15 minutes or until tender.
Drain and cool. Cut artichokes into halves or quarters,
depending on size. (Snip off any purple leaves.)

Mix together wine vinegar, oil, garlic powder, and pars-
ley. Add artichokes. Stir, cover, and refrigerate. (Better on
the second day.) Will keep several weeks in the refrigera-
tor; stir occasionally.

ARTICHOKE ZUCCHINI SAUTÉ

California Artichoke Advisory Board

Ingredients for 4 servings:
2 medium California artichokes
2 teaspoons minced garlic

1 teaspoon minced shallots
1 tablespoon each: olive oil and butter or margarine
2 cups sliced zucchini
1/4 cup dry white wine
3/4 teaspoon thyme
1/2 cup peeled, seeded, diced tomatoes
salt and pepper to taste

Cut artichokes into very thin lengthwise slices. Sauté artichokes, garlic, and shallots in olive oil and butter until artichokes are tender. Add zucchini, wine, and thyme. Cook 1 to 2 minutes or until zucchini is tender. Add tomatoes, salt, and pepper; cook until tomatoes are thoroughly heated.

(Preparation time: less than 30 minutes.)

NUTRIENTS PER SERVING

Calories...................... 102
Protein .... 2.9 g
Fat.............................. 6.3 g
Carbohydrates .... 7.6 g
Cholesterol .... 8.0 mg
Fiber .... 5.2 g
Sodium...................... 52.0 mg

BAKED GARLIC PARSNIPS

Vicki Rae Chelf
Cooking With the Right Side of the Brain
(Avery Publishing Group, 1991)

Ingredients for 2 to 4 servings:
1 to 2 tablespoons olive oil
4 to 8 small parsnips, scrubbed and sliced (2 to 3 cups)
3 or more garlic cloves, to taste, minced
2 tablespoons minced parsley
pinch of nutmeg
optional: pinch of sea salt

1. Place the oil in a shallow baking dish. Add the parsnips and the garlic. Stir to coat with the oil.
2. Cover the dish and bake at 350 degrees for about 30 minutes, or until the parsnips are tender. Stir from time to time and check for doneness.
3. Uncover and broil for a couple of minutes to lightly brown the parsnips. Toss with parsley and sprinkle with nutmeg. Add a pinch of sea salt if desired. (*Preparation time:* 35 minutes.)

GARLIC ROASTED CORN

James Levin, M.D., and Natalie Cederquist
A Celebration of Wellness
(Avery Publishing Group, 1992)

Ingredients per person:
1 ear white corn, with husk on
2 garlic cloves, sliced
1 lime wedge

Preheat oven to 500 degrees.

1. Soak corn in water (with husk on) for 15 to 20 minutes.
2. Peel back husk of corn, remove all corn silk, and wash corn cob. Rub corn with garlic, pull husk up around corn, and place garlic slices inside. Tie husks with string.
3. Place in oven and roast for 30 minutes; unhusk before serving. Squeeze lime over corn before eating.

This can also be cooked on a barbecue or grill if desired.

GRILLED GARLIC AND VEGETABLES

James Levin, M.D., and Natalie Cederquist
A Celebration of Wellness
(Avery Publishing Group, 1992)

Ingredients:
3 garlic bulbs, roasted (see Index for Roasted Garlic recipes)
1 each: green and red peppers, seeded and ribbed

4 green onions, tops and bottoms trimmed
1 small eggplant, sliced thinly lengthwise
extra virgin olive oil
lemon juice
cracked pepper
1 teaspoon oregano or basil
sea salt to taste

Preheat oven at 550 degrees.

1. Slice off bottom and top of peppers, then cut peppers into 3 slabs vertically.
2. Brush vegetables lightly with olive oil and lemon, place on a ventilated rack for oven broil or on a grill. Broil at 450 degrees for approximately 5 minutes, until softened. Put roasted whole garlics and vegetables on a platter. Sprinkle with herbs.

Serving suggestion: Arrange on a platter as a side dish; especially good with pasta.

SPAGHETTI SQUASH IN FRESH TOMATO SAUCE

Jacques Pépin
Jacques Pépin's Table (KQED Books, 1995)

We often enjoy spaghetti squash at our house and occasionally serve it as a low-calorie substitute for pasta. It doesn't taste like pasta, obviously, but its fresh flavor and crisp texture are complemented by pasta sauces. There are different ways of cooking spaghetti squash, but I think roasting it, as we do here, produces a great result and is especially easy.

For the delicious fresh tomato sauce served here with the squash, two heads of garlic are halved crosswise, wrapped in foil, and roasted alongside the squash. Then, when the cloves are soft and nicely browned on their cut edges, their tender flesh is squeezed out and added to a sauce composed of onion, fresh tomato pieces, and seasonings. Mild and tender, roasted garlic can also be served on its own or with other dishes.

Ingredients for 4 servings:
1 spaghetti squash (2-1/2 to 3 pounds)
2 teaspoons canola oil
2 heads garlic (about 6 ounces total)
3 tablespoons virgin olive oil
1 onion (about 4 ounces), peeled and chopped (1 cup)
3 or 4 ripe tomatoes (1 pound), cut into 2-inch pieces
1 teaspoon *herbes de Provence* or Italian seasoning
1-1/2 teaspoons salt
3/4 teaspoon freshly ground black pepper
1/3 cup water
1 tablespoon chopped fresh chives
optional: 2 or 3 tablespoons grated Parmesan cheese

1. Preheat the oven to 400 degrees.
2. Cut the squash in half crosswise, and scoop out the seeds with a spoon. Brush the cut side of the squash halves with 1 teaspoon of the canola oil, and place them cut side down on a cookie sheet or in a roasting pan.
3. Cut a rectangle of aluminum foil about 6-by-12 inches, and spread the remaining teaspoon of canola oil over half its surface. Cut the heads of garlic in half crosswise, and place them cut side down next to one another on the oiled half of the foil. Fold the unoiled half over the garlic, and fold the edges of the foil together tightly.
4. Place the foil package containing the garlic next to the squash halves on the cookie sheet or in the roasting pan, and bake at 400 degrees for 40 to 45 minutes. The squash should be tender when pierced with a knife, and its cut sides should be nicely browned; the garlic cloves should be soft throughout, and their cut surfaces should be nicely browned.
5. Heat 2 tablespoons of the olive oil until hot, but not smoking, in a medium saucepan. Add the onion, and sauté for 2 or 3 minutes. Add the tomatoes, *herbes de Provence* (or Italian seasoning), 1 teaspoon of the salt, and the pepper. Squeeze the soft garlic cloves out of their skins, and add

them to the saucepan. Mix well, add the water, and bring the mixture to a strong boil. Cover, and boil over high heat for 10 minutes. Then push the mixture through a food mill set over a saucepan. Set aside.

6. Using a fork, loosen and release the "spaghetti" strands from the squash halves, and mix them gently but thoroughly in a bowl with the remaining 1/2 teaspoon of salt and 1 tablespoon of olive oil.

7. At serving time, reheat the "spaghetti" until it is hot in a microwave oven for 1-1/2 to 2 minutes, or in a conventional oven set at 400 degrees for 10 to 12 minutes. Reheat the sauce in the saucepan until it is hot, and then ladle a large spoonful of it onto each of four dinner plates. Divide the "spaghetti" among the plates and drizzle about 1 tablespoon of the remaining sauce on top of each serving. Sprinkle with the chives, and serve immediately, with the cheese, if desired.

Spaghetti squash is a wonderful low-calorie alternative to pasta. Canola oil is the oil lowest in saturated fat, and Parmesan cheese is rich in calcium.

NUTRIENTS PER SERVING

Calories...................... 271
Protein .... 5 g
Carbohydrates .... 35 g
Fat.............................. 14.2 g
Saturated Fat............. 1.9 g
Cholesterol .... 0 mg
Sodium...................... 878 mg

GARLIC SPINACH SOUFFLÉ

Frieda's, Inc.

Ingredients for 5 or 6 servings:
1 tablespoon softened butter or margarine
1 tablespoon grated Parmesan cheese
1/4 cup butter or margarine

1 clove elephant garlic, minced (true garlic cloves may be substituted)
1/4 cup flour
1-1/4 cups milk
1/4 teaspoon ground red pepper
1/4 teaspoon salt
1 package (10 ounces) frozen chopped spinach, thawed
5 egg yolks
5 egg whites

Grease a 1-1/2 quart soufflé dish with the softened butter; sprinkle Parmesan inside dish. Set aside.

In a saucepan melt the 1/4 cup butter; add garlic and sauté over low heat for 2 minutes. Stir in flour, then add milk all at once. Stir in red pepper and salt. Cook and stir till thickened and bubbly. Remove from heat. Squeeze out all excess moisture from spinach. Place sauce and spinach in a food processor with blade, or in a blender.

Cover and process till smooth. (With blender, scrape down sides of container from time to time to make blending easier.) Return mixture to saucepan. Beat the egg yolks on high speed of electric mixer for about 5 minutes or till thick and lemon-colored. Stir some of the spinach mixture into yolks; then, gradually, add yolk mixture to sauce mixture, stirring to blend.

Wash beaters in hot soapy water. On high speed of electric mixer beat egg whites till stiff peaks form. Fold whites gently into spinach mixture until egg whites cannot be seen (do not stir). Turn mixture into soufflé dish. Bake in a 325-degree oven about 40 to 50 minutes, or till puffed and golden. Serve at once.

GLORIFIED GARLIC-LENTIL STEW

Northwest Garlic Festival
Ocean Park, Washington

Ingredients for 8 to 10 servings:
1/2 cup chopped garlic, packed tight

1-1/2 cups chopped onion (white)
1/4 cup butter or margarine
1 rounded teaspoon ground cumin seed

Sauté the (above) ingredients in covered skillet until very limp. In a large pot, combine this mixture and the following ingredients:

1 cup asparagus tips, cut 1/4 inch long
1 cup celery tops, chopped and packed
2/3 cup green onion tops, chopped and packed
1/2 cup broccoli stalks, chopped and packed
1 cup bell pepper, chopped and packed
1/2 cup cauliflower, chopped and packed
1/2 cup carrots, chopped and packed
3 cans (14.5 ounces each) clear low-salt chicken broth
optional: 12 black whole peppercorns
1 level teaspoon lemon pepper
1/2 cup lentils
1/2 cup black-eyed peas

Bring all ingredients to a boil in pot. Turn to low. Cook on stovetop 1-1/2 hours, stirring often. Put in 375-degree oven for 1 hour. Serve with fresh-baked garlic bread.

BROCCOLI AND GARLIC

The Garlic Information Center
New York Hospital-Cornell University Medical Center

Ingredients for 4 servings:
3 large stalks broccoli, ends trimmed
5 peeled garlic cloves, crushed
2 teaspoons olive oil
water for steaming
1/2 cup red wine (or substitute 1 tablespoon balsamic vinegar and 1/2 cup water)

1 small minced jalapeño
pepper to taste

*Sauté garlic in olive oil until lightly browned. Add chopped
jalapeño pepper and continue to sauté for another minute.
Pour red wine into sauté pan and allow to reduce for 1 to
2 minutes. Add the broccoli, cover, and simmer until the
broccoli is tender. If liquid evaporates before broccoli is
cooked, add a small amount of water.*

NUTRIENTS PER SERVING

Calories...................... 85
Protein .... 3 g
Fat............................. 3 g (28 percent)
Carbohydrates........... 7 g
Sodium...................... 48 mg

CLAY POT VEGETABLES

Diane Wilen

Ingredients:
4 red potatoes, in quarters
1 turnip, in chunks
3 celery stalks, in 3-inch pieces
4 carrots, in 2-inch chunks
2 onions, in chunks
1 head garlic, unpeeled, in cloves
whole mushrooms
2 to 3 tablespoons olive oil
2 bay leaves
pepper, thyme, parsley

*Soak the clay pot in water while you're shopping for the
ingredients.*

*Heat oven to 400 degrees. Toss vegetables, herbs, and
spices together with oil, and roast for 1 hour in clay pot.*

*An omelet without garlic is like a day without
sunshine.*

Dr. James Scala

TORTILLA CON VEGETABLES FRIJOLES

(Omelet With Garden Vegetables and Beans)
American Egg Board

To Mexicans, a tortilla is a thin, griddle-baked bread based on
flour or corn. To many other Spanish-speaking people, a tortilla is a pan-sized omelet made without stirring and served
open-faced. In any language, an omelet is a nutritious and
easy-to-make dish suited to any meal of the day.

Ingredients for 3 servings:
nonstick vegetable spray
1-1/2 cups sliced yellow summer squash or zucchini
3/4 cup chopped sweet red, yellow, or green pepper
1/2 cup chopped onion
2 tablespoons lime juice
1 can (15 ounces) pinto beans, rinsed and drained
3 eggs
1/3 cup skim or low-fat (1 percent) milk
1 teaspoon garlic powder

*Lightly coat 10-inch omelet pan or skillet with nonstick
spray. In pan, stir together squash, pepper, onion, and lime
juice. Cover and cook over medium heat until vegetables
are tender, about 4 to 5 minutes. Stir in beans.*

*In a small bowl, beat together eggs, milk, and garlic
powder until blended. Pour over vegetables. Cover and
cook over low heat until no visible liquid egg remains,
about 15 minutes.*

*Cut into wedges to serve from pan, or either slide from
pan or invert onto serving platter.*

NUTRIENTS PER SERVING OF 1/3 RECIPE
USING YELLOW SQUASH, RED PEPPER, AND SKIM MILK

Calories...................... 199
Protein .... 14 g
Total Fat.................... 6 g
Cholesterol .... 213 mg
Carbohydrates .... 23 g
Sodium...................... 310 mg

GARLIC CORNY CASSEROLE

"Garlicfest"
Fairfield, Connecticut

Ingredients for a 4-cup casserole:
2 cups whole kernel corn, fresh, cooked, or canned
1/2 small onion, chopped
2 cloves elephant garlic, chopped
optional: dash of ground red hot peppers
3/4 cup milk
1 cup Ritz cracker crumbs
3 tablespoons green bell pepper, chopped
salt and pepper to taste
2 tablespoons melted butter

Ingredients for crumb topping:
1/2 cup Ritz cracker crumbs
3/4 cup grated cheddar cheese

Combine corn, milk, and 1 cup cracker crumbs. Let stand 5 minutes. Add remaining casserole ingredients except butter. Pour into a 1-quart baking dish and dribble melted butter evenly over the top.

For the topping, mix the 1/2 cup cracker crumbs and cheese, and sprinkle over top. Bake in a preheated 350-degree oven for 30 minutes.

STIR-FRIED VEGETABLES

"Garlicfest"
Fairfield, Connecticut

Ingredients for a 4 to 6 servings:

2 tablespoons oil

2 pounds vegetables (asparagus, broccoli, carrots, green beans, pea pods, etc.)

2 tablespoons soy sauce

1/4 cup toasted nuts (cashews, almonds, etc.)

4 to 5 cloves garlic, peeled and minced

1 can (8 ounces) water chestnuts, drained and sliced

salt and pepper to taste

Heat oil in a large skillet or wok. Add garlic to oil. When the garlic begins to give off aroma, add vegetables and stir-fry over high heat until crisp-tender. Add water chestnuts and seasonings. Stir-fry another minute to heat through. Sprinkle with nuts and serve at once.

Eating garlic . . . Such pleasure! Such bliss! And the bliss begets awe, and the awe begets praise, and the praise begets appreciation for all that is, which, in turn, begets religion. Garlic proves there is God, for only an Omnipotent Being possesses that imagination to create garlic where once there was nothing. In the beginning was the Word and the Word found its perfect form in garlic.

Have I told you about my garlic shrine . . . ?

Stanley Hoffman

Appendices

Garlic Festivals

Dracula's loss; mankind's gain

Richard Sutor

Can you imagine a day or two of feasting on fabulous garlic-flavored food and not having to give your breath a second thought? That's what Garlic Festivals are all about. That and lots more, including popular garlic-related products (braids, wreaths, aprons, hats, posters, jewelry, roasters, keepers, peelers, etc.), and some products that you may not have known existed (garlic incense, garlic soap, garlic napkin holders, garlic bird houses, wind chimes made with garlic, and garlic on a leash).

At some of the festivals there are enlightening lectures, cooking contests, entertainment, garlic oil foot massages, and even psychic readings using garlic cloves. At all of the festivals there are great eats, lots of fun, and friendly, happy people. You'll be one of them when you visit any of the following:

Note: These have been, and hopefully will continue to be, ongoing festivals. It would be wise to call the contact number and find out the exact dates, times, and specific locations, so you can make travel plans to join the festivities.

MONTH OF MAY

GARLICFEST   203 / 372-6521
Fairfield, Connecticut

MONTH OF JUNE

NORTHWEST GARLIC FESTIVAL   360 / 665-5495
Ocean Park, Washington

MONTH OF JULY

WASHINGTON, D.C., GARLIC FESTIVAL   800 / RU GARLIC

LOS ANGELES GARLIC FESTIVAL   800 / 96 GARLIC
Los Angeles, California

GILROY GARLIC FESTIVAL   408 / 842-1625
Gilroy, California

Started in August 1979, the Gilroy Garlic Festival is not only the
oldest, but it's the biggest, attracting over 130,000 people annually. It is considered one of the country's top visitor events. The
Gilroy Garlic Festival is appropriately held in Gilroy, California,
the garlic capital of the world.

According to local legend, as Will Rogers was driving through
Gilroy at harvest time, he described it as "the only town in
America where you can marinate a steak just by hanging it out on
the clothesline."

MONTH OF AUGUST

ADAMS GARLIC FESTIVAL   860 / 599-4241
Pawcatuck, Connecticut

FOX RUN VINEYARDS GARLIC FESTIVAL   315 / 536-4616
Penn Yan, New York

WESTERN NEW YORK GARLIC FESTIVAL   716 / 637-6586
Batavia, New York

ARLINGTON GARLIC FESTIVAL   360 / 435-8577
Arlington, Washington

DEERFIELD VALLEY FARMERS MARKET   802 / 368-7147
GARLIC AND HERB FESTIVAL
Wilmington, Vermont

ARLEUX GARLIC FESTIVAL   French
(*FOIRE A AIL*)   Government
(Near the Belgian border)   Tourist Office
Arleux, France   New York, New York
                                       212 / 838-7800

MONTH OF SEPTEMBER

GARLICFEST   330 / 855-1141
Cleveland, Ohio

HUDSON VALLEY GARLIC FESTIVAL   914 / 246-5657
Saugerties, New York

MONTH OF OCTOBER

VIRGINIA GARLIC FESTIVAL   804 / 946-5168
Amherst, Virginia

Resources

Garlic is as good as ten mothers.

Telgu proverb of India

When looking for anything garlic, start with this list.

There are extraordinary food products and all kinds of unique garlic items. Although, in a few cases, we point out specialties, it would be impossible to mention each company's inventory. Instead, we urge you to call, fax, or write for free catalogs—each of them has one—and see for yourself.

CHRISTOPHER RANCH
Mail Order Department
305 Bloomfield Avenue
Gilroy, CA 95020

Tel: 800 / 957-5501
Fax: 800 / 637-2815

EVERYTHING GARLIC
Store:
Unit 122–123 Carrie Cates Court
Lonsdale Quay Market
North Vancouver, B.C. V7 M 3K7
For Canada catalog: P.O. Box 91104
West Vancouver, B.C. V7V 3N3
Canada

Tel: 800 / 668-6299
Fax: 604 / 926-3154

FILAREE FARM
182 Conconully Highway
Okanogan, WA 98840

Tel: 509 / 522-6940

Specialty: A tremendous selection of organic garlic varieties for growing. The catalog also offers artistic garlic novelty items: T-shirts, posters, etc.

GARLIC FESTIVAL FOODS
P.O. Box 1145
Gilroy, CA 95021-1145

Tel: 800 / 4 GARLIX
Tel: 888 / GARLICFEST
Fax: 408 / 842-7087

GARLIC GROCERY   Tel: 408 / 842-3330
8300 Arroyo Circle, Suite 330
Gilroy, CA 95020

GARLIC RESEARCH LABS   Tel: 800 / 424-7990
624 Ruberta Avenue
Glendale, CA 91201
Specialty: Garlic Barrier, insect repellent for home, garden, and agriculture. Also, Garlic Juice Spray for cooking.

THE GARLIC SHOPPE   Tel: 800 / 842-MAMA
P.O. Box 247   Fax: 408 / 842-8353
Gilroy, CA 95021
Specialty: Chateau De Garlic (garlic dinner wine) from their winery.

GARLIC WORLD   Tel: 800 / 537-6122
4800 Monterey Highway   Fax: 408 / 848-4278
Gilroy, CA 95020

GILROY GARLIC FESTIVAL ASSOCIATION
P.O. Box 2311   Tel: 408 / 842-1625
Gilroy, CA 95021-2311   Fax: 408 / 842-7337
(The Gilroy Garlic Festival is a once-a-year event, but their free catalog and products are available throughout the year.)

HÖSGOOD'S   Tel: 800 / 4 GARLIC
P.O. Box 1265   Fax: 713 / 933-9895
Stafford, TX 77497-1265

THE HOUSE OF GARLIC   Tel: 800 / RU GARLIC
63 East State Street   Fax: 215 / 340-9566
Doylestown, PA 18901

OMESSI GROUP LTD.   Tel: 818 / 831-0748
11710 Doral Avenue
Northridge, CA 91326
Specialty: Manufacturer of E-Z-Rol, the revolutionary rubber tube that makes peeling garlic cloves easy. Available at many stores

where kitchen gadgets are sold, or directly through the Omessi Group.

THE PIKLED GARLIK COMPANY   Tel: 800 / 775-9788
P.O. Box 846   Fax: 408 / 393-1709
Pacific Grove, CA 93950
Specialty: Pickled garlic and garlic salsa.

TV CHEFS—PROGRESSIVE GARLIC Tel: 800 / 288-7834
P.O. Box 84848   Fax: 206 / 233-0753
Seattle, WA 98124
(Progressive International Corp. has many products for storing and for preparing garlic. TV CHEFS will send Progressive's catalog upon request.)

If your interest in garlic goes beyond sprinkling powder on your pizza, you may want to consider membership in either or both of these organizations:

GARLIC SEED FOUNDATION:
Garlic Products ... Mail Order Companies and Stores

While the geneticists ponder why this plant would lose its sexuality, the botanists study garlic's variety and biological characteristics, and the chemists and medical researchers examine sulfur and its effect on our body, the Garlic Seed Foundation (GSF) seeks to answer the questions: How do you grow and eat this stinky stuff?

Created in 1984, the GSF is an international organization centered in Northeast United States. Our objectives are to educate, promote production and consumption of garlic using appropriate and sustainable practices, work with local members to organize festivals, and have some fun as we wear our breaths proudly.

GSF acts as a clearinghouse of research data; presents educational seminars to consumers, farmers, gardeners, and horticulturists; and fills a neutral information void without consideration for sale of pills or products.

The newsletter, the *Garlic Press*, is published about four times a year. For membership information, send a self-addressed, stamped envelope to:

> David Stern
> Garlic Seed Foundation
> Rose Valley Farm
> Rose, NY 14542-0149

GARLIC LOVERS ASSOCIATION

The mission of the Garlic Lovers Association is to bring together the interests of consumers, retailers, and growers around the world to further the cause of garlic as a food, a natural cure-all, and a means to bring great numbers of people together to celebrate nonconformity, fun, and togetherness.

For membership information, send a self-addressed, stamped envelope to:

> Garlic Lovers Association
> 63 East State Street
> Doylestown, PA 18901

READERS WISHING TO CONTACT THE AUTHORS can write to Lydia or Joan Wilen at:

> Joan Wilen & Lydia Wilen
> P.O. Box 419
> Ansonia Station
> New York, NY 10023-0416

Bibliography

Aaron, Chester. *Garlic Is Life* (Ten Speed Press, 1996)

Adams, Rex. *Miracle Medicine Foods* (Parker Publishing Company, Inc., 1977)

Allison, Christine. *365 Days of Gardening* (HarperCollins, 1995)

Bader, Dr. Myles H. *6001 Food Facts and Chef's Secrets* (Northstar Publishing Company, 1995)

Bergner, Paul. *The Healing Power of Garlic* (Prima Publishing, 1996)

Bricklin, Mark. *The Practical Encyclopedia of Natural Healing* (Rodale Press, Inc., 1983)

Buchman, Dian Dincin, Ph.D. *Herbal Medicine* (Wings Books, 1996)

Burtis, C. Edward. *Nature's Miracle Medicine Chest* (Arco Publishing Company, Inc., 1974)

Carper, Jean. *Food—Your Miracle Medicine* (HarperCollins, 1993)

Carper, Jean. *Stop Aging Now!* (HarperCollins, 1995)

Castleman, Michael. *The Healing Herbs* (Bantam Books, 1995)

Clement, Brian R., with Theresa Foy DiGeronimo. *Living Foods for Optimum Health* (Prima Publishing, 1996)

Cochrane, Peggy. *The Sorcerers' Guide to Good Health* (Barricade Books, Inc., 1993)

Colbin, Annemarie. *Food and Healing* (Ballantine Books, 1996)

Crawford, Stanley. *A Garlic Testament* (HarperCollins, 1992)

Cunningham, Scott. *The Magic in Food* (Llewellyn Publications, 1992)

De Lys, Claudia. *What's So Lucky About a Four-Leaf Clover?* (Bell Publishing Company, 1989)

Engeland, Ron L. *Growing Great Garlic—The Definitive Guide for Organic Gardeners and Small Farmers* (Filaree Productions, 1991)

Fulder, Stephen, and John Blackwood. *Garlic—Nature's Original Remedy* (Healing Arts Press, 1991)

Gardner, Joy. *The New Healing Yourself* (The Crossing Press, 1989)

Giller, Robert M., M.D., and Kathy N. Matthews. *Natural Prescriptions* (Carol Southern Books, 1994)

Gottlieb, Bill. *New Choices in Natural Healing* (Rodale Press, 1995)

Harris, Ben Charles. *Kitchen Medicines* (Pocket Books, 1968)

Harris, Lloyd J. *The Book of Garlic* (Aris Books, 1979)

Heinerman, John, Ph.D. *The Healing Benefits of Garlic* (Keats Publishing, Inc., 1994)

Herbst, Sharon Tyler. *The Food Lover's Tiptionary* (William Morrow and Company, 1994)

Jackson, Mildred, N.D., and Terri Teague. *The Handbook of Alternatives to Chemical Medicine* (Lawton-Teague Publications, 1975)

Jensen, Bernard, Ph.D. *Garlic Healing Powers* (Bernard Jensen, Ph.D., 1992)

Kim, Andrew H.Y. *Discover Natural Health* (Kim's Publishing, 1988)

Koch, Heinrich P., Ph.D., M. Pharm., and Larry D. Lawson, Ph.D. *Garlic—The Science and Therapeutic Application of* Allium sativum L. *and Related Species* (Williams & Wilkins, 1996)

Kordel, Lelord. *Natural Folk Remedies* (Manor Books, Inc., 1974)

Lasne, Sophie, and Andre Pascal Gaultier. *A Dictionary of Superstitions* (Prentice Hall, Inc., 1984)

Lau, Benjamin, M.D., Ph.D. *Garlic for Health* (Lotus Light Publications, 1988)

Lin, Dr. Robert I-San. *Garlic in Nutrition & Medicine* (International Health Promotions, 1989)

Logan, Patrick. *Irish Country Cures* (Sterling Publishing Company, Inc., 1994)

Lucas, Richard. *Common & Uncommon Uses of Herbs for Healthful Living* (Arco Publishing, Inc., 1982)

Lucas, Richard. *Herbal Health Secrets* (Parker Publishing Company, Inc., 1983)

Lust, John. *The Herb Book* (Bantam Books, 1974)

Mairesse, Michelle. *Health Secrets of Medicinal Herbs* (Arco Publishing, Inc., 1981)

Margen, Sheldon, M.D., and the Editors of the University of California at Berkeley *Wellness Letter. The Wellness Encyclopedia of Food and Nutrition* (Rebus, 1992)

McGrath, William R. *Amish Folk Remedies* (Amish Acres, 1985)

Mosby Medical Encyclopedia (New American Library, 1985)

Ni, Maoshing, Ph.D., C.A., with Cathy McNease, B.S., M.H. *The Tao of Nutrition* (The Shrine of the Eternal Breath of Tao, and College of Tao and Traditional Chinese Healing, 1987)

Peterson, Vicki. *The Book of Healthy Foods* (St. Martin's Press, 1981)

Petulengro, Leon. *The Roots of Health* (Signet Books, 1968)

Polunin, Miriam, and Christopher Robbins. *The Natural Pharmacy* (Collier Books, 1992)

Riccio, Dolores. *Superfoods* (Warner Books, 1992)

Rodale, J.I., and Staff. *The Complete Book of Food and Nutrition* (Rodale Press, 1961)

Rose, Jeanne. *Herbs & Things* (Perigee Books, 1972)

Roséan, Lexa. *The Supermarket Sorceress* (St. Martin's Press, 1996)

St. Claire, Debra. *Herbal Preparations and Natural Therapies: Creating and Using a Home Herbal Medicine Chest*, Video Instruction, Reference/Resource Manual, and Pocket Herbal Reference Guide (Morningstar Publications 800/435-1670 303/444-6072)

Scala, Dr. James. *Prescription for Longevity* (Dutton, 1992)

Simpson, Caryl. *International Garlic Festival Cookbook* (Gourmet Gold Press, 1994)

Thomas, Lalitha. *Ten Essential Herbs* (Hohm Press, 1995)

Tyler, Varro E., Ph.D. *Herbs of Choice* (Pharmaceutical Products Press, 1994)

Vogel, Dr. H.C.A. *Swiss Nature Doctor* (A. Vogel, Switzerland, 1980)

Von Hausen, Wanja. *Gypsy Folk Medicine* (Sterling Publishing Co., Inc.)

Wade, Carlson. *Health Secrets From the Orient* (Parker Publishing Company, Inc., 1973)

Wade, Carlson. *Nutritional Healers* (Parker Publishing Company, Inc., 1987)

Walker, Morton, D.P.M. *The Healing Powers of Garlic* (New Way of Life, Inc., 1988)

Weil, Andrew, M.D. *Spontaneous Healing* (Alfred A. Knopf, 1995)

Wilen, Joan, and Lydia Wilen. *Chicken Soup & Other Folk Remedies* (Fawcett Columbine, 1984)

Wilen, Joan, and Lydia Wilen. *Folk Remedies That Work* (HarperPerennial, 1996)

Wilen, Joan, and Lydia Wilen. *More Chicken Soup & Other Folk Remedies* (Fawcett Columbine, 1986)

Williams, Jude C., M.H. *Jude's Herbal Home Remedies* (Llewellyn Publications, 1992)

Winter, Ruth, M.S. *A Consumer's Guide To Medicines In Food* (Crown Trade Paperbacks, 1995)

Index

A

Absorption, 46
Acupuncture, 9
Adverse reactions, 27
   headache, 64
   skin, 57
   stomach irritation, 25
Aging fresh bulbs, 126
Aioli sauce, 136
Air pollution, 82
Aliens' gift, 10
Allergies, 31, 95
   allergy-ease tonic, 31
   hay fever, 64
Allicin, 23, 40, 48, 65
Anemia, iron treatment for, 116-117
Angina pectoris, 65
Anti-infection wash, 117-118
Antibiotic, 21-22, 23, 25, 70
   animal bites, 33-34
   formula, 106
   impetigo, 68
   skin infections, 70
   wash, 108
Anticoagulant, 38
Antidepressant, 49-50
Antitoxin, 31
Aphrodisiac, 69
Appetite control, 91
Appetite restorer for horses, 96
Arterial plaque, 65
Arthritis in animals, 96-97
Arthritis liniment, formula for, 117-118
Athlete's foot, 56-57, 107
Autoimmunodeficiency (AIDS), 31

B

Bandages, 58-59, 111
Baptism, 17
Bathing
   footbath, 107
   for insomnia, 72
   garlic baths, 106
   personal protection spell, 12
Bladder infection (cystitis), 49

Blood
   anemia, 33
   blood thinner, 34, 38
   clots, 37-38
   pressure, 38-40
   red blood cells, 37
   strengthening formula, 116
   See also cardiovascular system.
Bloody nose, 80
Botulism, 110, 132
Braiding, 18, 126
Breath fresheners, 59-60
Bronchitis and asthma tea, 116
Bubonic plague, 14
Buchman, Dian Dincin, 45
   arthritis liniment formula, 117-118
Bug repellent, 71-72

C

Calories, 138
Cancer, 42-43, 75-76
   in animals, 97
   prostate, 84
Candidiasis, 94-95
Cardiovascular system, 34, 65-66
Chicago named for, 9
Chicken soup, 45-46
Cholera, 13
Cholesterol, 43-44
Chopping, 134
Christopher Ranch, 18, 230
Clement, Brian and Anna Maria, 26,
      43, 93
Colds, 44-45
Colic in infants, 83
Congestion, 47-48
   lung, 80
   nasal, 78-79
Constipation in horses, 97
Corns on the foot, 57
Cortisone, 35-36
Cough syrup, 112
Coughs, 41
   in animals, 98
   with congestion, 47-49
Cracking (popping) the bulb, 133

Cultivation, history, 4, 11-12,
Curing fresh bulbs, 126
Cystitis, 49

D

Daily regimen, 25
  hypertension, 39
  immune system, 67-68
  prevention of stroke, 88
Dandruff treatment, 61
Decongestant, 32
Dental remedies, 61, 89
Depression, 49-50
Diabetes, 50
Diallyl sulfides, 14, 65
Digestive enzymes, 52
Digging up bulbs, 125
Dog biscuits, 99-100
Dosage
  general, 21-22
  powdered and fresh equivalents, 25
  veterinary uses, 96
Dreams, 16-17, 80
Drowsiness, 55-56
Dysbiosis, 52
Dysentery, prevention of, 51
  enema for, 107

E

Ear mites, 100
Ear problems, 53-55
Earwax buildup, 54
Eczema, dogs and cats, 100
Emergency bandaging, 58-59, 111
Enema, 47-48, 92
  herbal cleanser, 107
Energy-boost food additive for pets,
  102
Enteric coated supplements, 24, 39-40
Enzymes for digestion, 52
Erections, 69

F

Festivals, 227-229
Fever, 57-58
Fingernail fungus, 89
Flea treatment for pets, 100
Flu, 44-45
Fluid retention, 39
Folk legends, 9, 11, 14, 16, 18
  warts, 90

Foot ailments, 36, 56-57, 107
Four Thieves Vinegar, 14-15
Freezing, 132
Fungus, 73
  athlete's foot, 56-57
  fingernail, 89
  male itch, 73
  ringworm, 84
  toenail, 89
  yeast-like, 94-95

G

Garlic breath, 59
Garlic juice, 109
Garlic lotion for hair growth, 61
Garlic Lovers Association, 233
Garlic maple syrup, 36
Garlic oil, 22, 110
  foot massage, 111
  for burns, 41-42
  for children's earache, 54
  for hemorrhoids, 66
  rub for arthritis, 35
  storage precautions, 110
Garlic pesticide, 127
Garlic salt, 137
Garlic sauce, 136
Garlic Seed Foundation, 232
Garlic smell, skin and hair, 106
Garlic syrup, 87, 112
Garlic tea compress, 88
Garlic Valley Farms, 75-76
Garlic varieties, 123, 131
Garlic vinegar, 57, 117
  with thyme, 71
Garlic water, 108
Garnish, 136
Gazpacho for hangover, 63
Genital herpes, 67
Genital itching, 73, 90
Gilroy Garlic Festival, 163, 228, 231
Gingivitis, 61
Gout, dietary regimen, 60
Greens, growing instructions, 126-127
Gynecological problems, 77-78

H

Hair growth, 62
Hangover remedy, 63
Harvesting homegrown, 125

Hawthorn with garlic for heart strength, 66
Headaches with "pinging," 65
Hearing loss, 54
Heartburn, 52
Hepatitis prevention, 66
Herbal tea, 115-116
Herpes, 67
High blood pressure, 38-40
High-density lipoproteins, 43-44
Hippocrates Health Institute, 26, 43
Hippocrates, 11
Histamines, 31
History of cultivation, 4, 11-12, 13
    Chinese, 12, 13
    Egyptians, 13
    Normans, 13
Hoffman, Dr. Ronald, 25-26, 34
Home blood pressure monitor, 40
Homegrown, 121-127
Huang-ti, Emperor, 12
Human Immunodeficiency Virus (HIV), 31
Hypertension, 38
    monitors, 40
    stroke, 88

I

Immune system, 31, 67-68
    immune-boosting power-packed potion, 68
Impotence test, 69
Indigestion, 52
Infants, nursing, 41, 83
Infection, 21
    antibiotic wash, 117-118
    dogs and cats, 101
    gums, 61
    prostate, 83-84
    sinus, 85
    throat, 86
    urinary (cystitis), 49
Inflammation of lymph glands, 75
Insect bites, 71
    dogs and cats, 101
Insect repellent, 71, 72
Intestinal inflammation, 47
Intestinal parasites, 92
Iron deficiency, 33
Iron tonic, 116
Irregularity, 48

Itch mites in pets, 102
Itch remedy, poison ivy, 81
Itching
    jock itch, 73
    rectal, 92
    relief, 71
    vaginal, 90

J

Jaundice in animals, 101
Jock itch, 73

L

Labor and pregnancy, 11, 82-83
Large intestine, inflammation, 47
Laryngitis, 87
Lawson, Dr. Larry, 24, 25
Lead poisoning, 73
"leaky gut" syndrome, 52
Leprosy, 11
Life change centers, 43
Liniment
    for arthritic joints, 35, 109
    anti-infection wash, 117
Linoleic acids, 83
Liver disease in cats and dogs, 101
Liver flush, 74
Living foods program, 43
    See also Clement, Brian and Anna Maria.
Longevity, 67-68
Love potion, 13-14
Low-density lipoproteins, 43-44
Lung congestion, 80
Lyme disease, 74

M

Mammary glands, 75
Mange, canine, 102
Massaging oil, 111
Melanoma, 75-76
Memory enhancement, 77
Menstrual cramps, 78
Merchandise, 227, 230-232
Mickaharic, Draja, *A Century of Spells,* 12
Migraines, 64
Miso-pickled garlic, 26
Mitogenetic radiation, 83
Molto fino, 45
Morning sickness, 83

Mosquito repellent, 71
Mouth infection, 88
Mulching garlic beds, 125

N

Neck pain, 79
Nerve swelling, 84
Nosedrops, 64, 85, 78
Nutritional values, 138

O

Odor on surfaces, 138
Odorless supplements, 24
Open sores, 93
Origin of word *garlic,* 4

P

Parasites, 91, 92, 95
    enema for, 107
    worms in cats and dogs, 102
Peelgarlic, 11
Peeling, 133
Percutaneous absorption, 46
Pescatore, Dr. Fred, 35, 70
Pets, 96-102
    tonic food additive, 102
Phytochemicals, 43
Pickled garlic, 26
Plantar warts, 91
Planting bulbs, 121-124
Poison from heavy metals, 73
Porphyria, 14
Poultice, 21, 33, 111
    pneumonia, 81
    skin infection, 70
    stiff neck, 79
    wounds, 93
Pregnancy, 82-83
Premenstrual syndrome (PMS), 76
Preparation for eating, 133-136
Pressing, 135
Prevention of
    bad breath, 60
    cancer, 42-43
    dysentery, 51
    ear infection, 53
    gangrene, 58-59
    hepatitis, 66
    infection, 21, 92-93
    lyme disease, 74
    poison ivy, 81

stroke, 88
Prostate cancer, 84
Protection from evil, 12, 16

R

Raw garlic intolerance, 25-26
Recipes
    Air Force One's secret applesauce, 192
    Appaloosa bean and fennel salad, 147
    artichoke zucchini saute, 213
    artichokes, marinated, 213
    bagel chips, garlic and herb, 161
    bagna calda, 196
    beef and vegetable fried rice, 155
    black bean chicken salad, 168
    broccoli and garlic, 220
    bronchitis and asthma tea, 116
    brown rice black bean burrito, 148
    bruschetta, 158, 159
    Caesar dressing, reduced fat, 197
    chalupa, 156
    chicken, 40-clove garlic, 169-172
    chicken, garlic and thyme with spinach, 166
    chicken, glazed xian, 167
    chicken, thai me up, 172
    chipp chicken, 165
    clay pot vegetables, 221
    corn, roasted, 215
    couscous, walnut lemon, 151
    creamy vinaigrette, 199
    croutons, italian walnut, 164
    elephant steaks, 154
    enhanced garlic formula, 105
    fiesta meat balls piquante, 155
    fish chili with garlic, 173
    fish, baked with walnut-coriander chutney, 175
    foccacia bread, easy elephant garlic, 160
    fritters, 144
    garlic basil custard, 141
    garlic beef soup, long beach, 186
    garlic chicken soup, 46
    garlic chip cookies, 201
    garlic chowder, 185
    garlic corny casserole, 223
    garlic herb salad dressing, fat free, 198

garlic juice, 109
garlic maple syrup, 36
garlic oxymel syrup, 113-114
garlic rice salad, 149
garlic soup, 185
garlic toast, 158
garlic vinaigrette, 198
garlic-lentil stew, 219-220
garlic-miso super soup, 111
garlic-mushroom stuffed sirloin, 152
garlic-sage tea, 87
garlicky dog biscuits, 99
gazpacho for hangover, 63
golden garlic clouds, 163
grilled garlic and vegetables, 215
guacamole, 194-195
guacamole, new-age, 208
honey-luscious garapple pie, 200
ice cream, holiday garlic, 203
immune boosting power-packed potion, 68
Italian ziti bake, 182
lamb loin, garlic-rubbed, 157
linguine with tuna, 177
macaroni salmon loaf, 176
marmalade, 192
muffins, mama mia, 162
paella, southwest vegetable, 150
parsley-garlic dip and spread, 196
parsnips, baked, 214
pasta delight, garlic-lovers', 189
pasta hoppin' John, 181
pasta primavera, 179
pasta with zucchini, 180
peanut-barley stuffing, 151
peppercorn tofu, 207
piperade/spanish sauce, 191
popcorn balls, 205
potatoes, catalan, 210
potatoes, garlic mashed, 211
potatoes, Nicoise, 212
prawns, Spanish style, 178
presto pesto, 193
ratatouille, 209
red pepper garlic pasta sauce, 190
roasted garlic, 197
Ron's rub, 199
salsa di molto aglio, 188
Sicilian gems, 204
skordalia, 193

snapper, garlic-crusted with shrimp, 174
soothing garlic syrup, 112
sopa de ajo, 184
soup, cold garlic, 183
space syrup, 10-11
spaghetti squash in fresh tomato sauce, 216-218
spinach souffle, 218
Spot's stew, 98-99
steak with parmesan-grilled vegetables, 153
stir-fried vegetables, 224
stuffed mushrooms, 146
sunflower snaps, 206
sweet potatoes, mashed, 212
thyme garlic vinegar, 71
tomato and risotto bisque, 187
tortilla con vegetables frijoles, 222
Uncle Ronnie's garlic cheesecake, 201
uncooked tomato sauce for pasta, 191
veggie pâté, 145
walnut crisps, 205
whole roasted garlic, 142-143
Rectal itching, 92
Red blood cells, See blood.
Reflux, 53
Refrigeration, 132
Repellent for garden pests, 122-123
Reproductive system
    female, 76-78, 82-83, 90
    male, 69, 83-84,
Respiratory tract, 31, 35-36, 41, 45
    effects of pollution, 82
    pneumonia, 80
Ringing in ears, 55
Ritkiss, Lavinia, 10
Roasting, 135-136, 142-143

S

Salad flavoring, 137
Salt in the diet, 39
Sautéing, 135
Schweitzer, Dr. Albert, 13
Sciatic nerve, 84
Seedbulbs, 123
Sexual desire, 69
Shopping for garlic, 131
Sinus infection, 85-86

Skin
  cancer, 76
  conditions in animals, 100
  infections
    cellulitis, 70
    impetigo, 68
    rashes, 70
  irritations, garlic vinegar prepara-
    tion, 117
  psoriasis, 84
  ringworm, 84
  sunburn, 88
Sleeplessness, 72
Smell, cleansing from hands, 137-138
Smog, 82
Snakes, 11
Sneezing, chronic, 86
Soil for growing, 122
Space syrup, 10-11
Spasms, 78, 80
Spells, 12, 16
Spots in eyes, 55
Sprouts, 126, 132
Stinking Lily, 4, 9
Stomach irritation, 25
Storage, 131-132
Stress, 79-80
Stroke prevention, 88

T

Talmud, 15-16
Teeth, painful, 89
Thomas, Lalitha, *Ten Essential Herbs,*
    21-22, 33, 47-48, 59, 105
Throat lozenges, 113, 114
Throat, 86-87

Tick repellent, 74
Ticks, treatment for pets, 100
Toenail infection, 89
Tonsils, 87
Translation to other languages, 4-6
Typhus, 13

V

Vampires, 14
Varieties, 131
Vinaigre des Quatres Voleurs, "Four
    Thieves Vinegar," 15
Vitamins, 33, 55
  for pollution, 82

W

Wade, Carlson, 31
  iron tonic formula, 116
  on hemoglobin, 37
  on prostate infection, 83
Wart removal, 90-91
Watercress, 40, 50
Weeding garlic beds, 125
Worms, 91-92, 102

Y

Yeast infections, 94-95
  thrush, 88
Yields, 137
Yogurt, 25-26, 107

Z

Ziment, Irwin, M.D., 45-46
  garlic chicken soup, 45-46
Zodiac signs and planting, 122